The Ugly Man

Kate Ryan as Veronica, Shaun Johnston as Forest.

THE UGLY MAN

BY
BRAD FRASER

Prairie Play Series: 13 • Series Editor, Diane Bessai

Canadian Cataloguing in Publication Data

Fraser, Brad, 1959-
  The ugly man

(Prairie play series ; 13)
ISBN 0-920897-43-6

  I. Title. II. Series.

PS8561.R294U45 1993   C812'.54   C93-090445-1
PR9199.3.F73U45 1993

Printed and bound in Canada by Hignell Printers Limited
NeWest Publishers Limited
201, 8540-109 Street
Edmonton, Alberta
T6G 1E6

CREDITS
Editor for the Press: Diane Bessai; Editorial Assistant: Don Perkins
Cover design: Brian Huffman
Interior design: Bob Young/BOOKENDS DESIGNWORKS
Photographs: Lawrence Herzog/Quest Communications – Workshop West
    production, February 1993
Financial Assistance: NeWest gratefully acknowledges the financial assistance of The
    Canada Council; The Alberta Foundation for the Arts, a beneficiary of the Lottery
    Fund of the Government of Alberta; and The NeWest Institute for Western
    Canadian Studies.

(Prairie Play Series Number 13)

Every effort has been made to obtain permission for photographs. If there is an omission or error the editors and publisher would be grateful to be so informed.

For Vern and Guy

OTHER BRAD FRASER PLAYS PUBLISHED BY NEWEST PRESS

The Wolf Plays, including *Wolfboy* and *Prom Night of the Living Dead*

TABLE OF CONTENTS

∎

Foreword

by Paula Simons[*]

When *The Ugly Man* first opened in Calgary in 1992, one of the local drama critics, dismissed it as "theatre for the *MuchMusic* generation."

Well, I am a member of the *MuchMusic* generation. And at the time, that glib assessment made me angry. I'd felt, and seen, the visceral impact this play had on audiences, and I'd seen how easily audiences connected to this challenging piece of theatre.

But the more I think about *The Ugly Man*, the more I realize – it *is* theatre for the *MuchMusic* generation. And that's what makes it so fascinating.

After all – why does anybody to go to live theatre these days? Especially anybody under 30? Thanks to modems and VCRs and compact discs and cable TV and satellite dishes, there's no need for people to leave home to be entertained. Going to the theatre isn't cheap. And seeing a new Canadian play is a gamble. What if you spend all that money to see something you won't like? Especially when you can watch ten hours of *Star Trek* a week without leaving your basement?

So ask yourself. Why *are* you reading this play? And why *are* thousands of people around the world going to

[*]Paula Simons is a documentary and features producer with CBC Radio in Edmonton. Her work is heard on programs such as "The Arts Tonight", "Ideas", and "Arts National". She has also written on the arts and popular culture for *Alberta Report*, *West Magazine*, *Western Living*, and *The Edmonton Journal*.

theatres to see *The Ugly Man* and other plays by Brad Fraser?

Because Brad Fraser has figured out how to keep theatre alive, how to attract new audiences, by writing in a pop cult idiom they can understand.

Sure, *The Ugly Man* has an elegant pedigree. It's based on a Jacobean revenge tragedy called *The Changeling*, by Thomas Middleton (1570?-1627) and William Rowley (1585?-1626), a story of lust and murder amongst decadent lords and ladies. But this story has nothing to do with 17th century England and everything to do with the two worlds in which Brad Fraser grew up.

The universe of *The Ugly Man* is vicious, disturbing, out-of-control. But if the play's gaudy horrors are sometimes absurd, the anger and terror they express are always real.

Brad Fraser grew up poor. He grew up abused, both physically and sexually. He grew up gay in a homophobic world. He grew up an intellectual changeling in a blue-collar world. He grew up angry. And he's put his own anger, his own personal experiences with violence and terror and prejudice and the abuse of power into the universe of this play.

But Brad Fraser also grew up in a world of books and comics and TV shows and old movies. He read whatever he could get his hands on. Superhero comic books. Horror comics. *Archie Comics*. The complete works of Harold Robbins. He watched television programs like *Batman* and *The Munsters* and *The Big Valley*. (Remember *The Big Valley*? It was a western that starred a pre-bionic Lee Majors, with Barbara Stanwyck as the wealthy and ruthless matriarch – Pa Cartwright in a leather skirt.)

TV also introduced Brad Fraser to lots and lots of old movies, re-run on those long-gone afternoon movie programs with names like *Siesta Cinema* and *The Big Money Movie*. Long before Brad Fraser discovered "high culture," the world of live theatre and Jacobean revenge tragedies, he had immersed himself in the idioms and images of the popular culture of the late 20th century.

And that's one of the reasons behind the popular success of *The Ugly Man*. These days, a playwright can't count on theatre audiences to know the Bible. Or Greek mythology. Or Shakespeare. When Shakespeare wrote plays, for example, he knew that everyone in his audience, from the groundlings to the aristocrats, shared a common knowledge of the stories of the Bible. Today, an author can't expect the audience to be culturally literate, in the classic sense. So where does a playwright find the symbols, the metaphors, the literary shorthand he needs to reach his audience? Especially an audience with an attention span shortened by rock videos, remote controls, and the fast-forward button on the VCR?

Brad Fraser found the symbols he needed. In the TV shows, the comic books, and the old movies he watched as a child. *The Ugly Man* may be patterned on a 17th century revenge tragedy, but almost every scene is inspired by a well-known scene from a movie or TV show: *Gone with the Wind. Double Indemnity. A Streetcar Named Desire. Mildred Pierce. Star Wars. The Fugitive. The Big Valley.*

And the play's characters are also pop cult reincarnations. *The Ugly Man* is not an exercise in prairie naturalism. Characterization doesn't count for much. The inhabitants of Brad Fraser's nightmare world are simply the agents of his whirlwind, macabre plot. And pop cult references allow him to sketch his characters quickly, so he can concentrate on crafting a work that moves as fast as any rock video, with enough jolts to serve the adrenalin needs of the most frenetic channel surfer. Pop cult shorthand gives Fraser an easy, subversive way to sneak in his big themes – the abuse of power, and the confusion of lust with love.

So Forest, the ugly hired man with the scarred face, is a kind of human monster, straight from the pages of *EC* horror comics. Veronica, the beautiful heartless bride, gets her name from Veronica Lodge, the hard-hearted heiress of the *Archie Comics*. And Sabina, Veronica's powerful scheming mother, simply *is* Barbara Stanwyck from *The Big Valley*.

Take Veronica. In the world of *Archie Comics*, Veronica Lodge isn't actually evil. She's a poor little rich girl, who flirts with Archie one minute, then decides he's too poor to be worth her attention the next. She's the most beautiful, popular girl in school – and an eternal virgin.

Fraser's Veronica takes those comic book traits to the extreme. She has no capacity for love, not even the ability to enjoy a normal sexual relationship. She has no affection for anyone. Not for her mother, not for her maid, Lottie, not for Acker, not even for Cole, Acker's disturbingly handsome best man. She only responds to Forest's sadistic sexual energies.

And in the end, every character in the play makes the same mistake as Veronica. They all confuse love with lust. The lust for power. The lust for revenge. The lust for romance. And of course, the lust for sexual conquest and sexual satisfaction.

Similarly, Fraser uses *The Big Valley* image of Barbara Stanwyck to explore his ideas about the abuse of power. Sabina, the matriarch of this universe, rules her ranch, her servants, and her community with an iron will. She bribes, buys, and controls everyone. When people finally rebel against Sabina's tyranny, the corrupt world she has created falls apart, with horrifying results. One by one, the other residents of the ranch try to fill the power vacuum, by grabbing for power themselves. One by one, they are destroyed, either physically or spiritually, by the power they sought.

And while the world of *The Ugly Man* collapses in violence and death, how are we supposed to react? Do we cry, or scream, or laugh? *The Ugly Man* gives audiences a sickening sense of vertigo. This is not comedy or horror. It is a disturbing and disorienting blend of the two. Again, Brad Fraser relies on the icons and images and echoes of popular culture to create his ironic tilt-o-whirl.

"I have a bad feeling about this." That's what Veronica tells her mother after Acker, Veronica's rich fiancé, discovers Veronica and Cole, the best man, in passionate embrace. No wonder. After all, Acker has run off into the woods. And Veronica has made a deal with Forest, the ugly man, to make sure that Acker never comes back.

It ought to be a horrible moment. Except that Veronica is speaking one of Han Solo's most memorable (and quoted) lines from the film *Star Wars*, one of the most popular movies of all time. And Brad Fraser can pretty safely assume that most of the people in his audiences will catch the echo of the line, even if they don't recognize or place it right away.

The result is the kind of ironic juxtaposition that makes the earth shift under your feet. One moment, you're caught up in the horror of the story. The next, you want to giggle at the incongruous image of Harrison Ford fighting the bad guys aboard the "Millenium Falcon."

When Brad Fraser himself directed a recent production of *The Ugly Man* in Edmonton, he highlighted this effect by having Lottie, the mysterious maid, sing a constant background chorus of Karen Carpenter's greatest (and most banal) hits. The easy-listening tunes and their inane lyrics made an absurd counterpoint to the evil and the eroticism on the stage. When Lottie burst into "We've Only Just Begun," the audience's giggles provided a release from what might otherwise have been the unbearable tension of the play.

Somehow, the playwright's subversive humour makes the terrors of the play more terrible. There's no doubt that contemporary theatre-goers have been desensitized to death and violence and eroticism by what they've seen in movies, on rock videos, even on the TV news. By using pop cult references to keep his audience on a constant roller coaster of laughter and horror, Brad Fraser is able to shake and shock his jaded audience into the emotional response he wants.

And audiences all over the world are responding to Brad Fraser and his plays. He's made waves and drawn crowds in Chicago and New York and Edinburgh and London. He's been translated into German and Italian and Japanese. As I write this, *The Ugly Man* is finishing a successful run, in French, in Montreal. A Calgary theatre company, One Yellow Rabbit, is taking it on tour to Edinburgh. Meanwhile, film-maker Denys Arcand is putting the finishing touches on a movie version of Brad Fraser's earlier hit *Unidentified Human Remains and the True Nature of Love*. And *Remains* is scheduled to get its Japanese stage première in Tokyo in the fall of 1993.

But Brad Fraser grew up – and wrote his plays – thousands of miles away from the big theatre centres like New York and London. Yet audiences around the world respond to his plays – because pop cult is the new *lingua franca*.

Fraser's audience is the first to come of age in a true global village. The blue-collar suburb where Brad Fraser grew up was light-years away from Barbara Stanwyck's Big Valley or Archie Andrew's Riverdale High. But for a nascent playwright, those alternate universes were as important and as real as Edmonton's snow and shopping malls. And that means any 25 year old, who grew up with American popular culture, in Tokyo or Buenos Aires or Minot or Aberdeen, will "get" *The Ugly Man*.

Of course, all those references to comic books and TV shows, all those rock video jump-cut techniques, drive some of the more senior members of the theatre establishment crazy. I recently had a rather heated argument with a leading Canadian artistic director, who suggested Brad Fraser's plays were no more than inferior sitcom scripts adapted for the stage.

"I never watch television," he sniffed. Well, Brad Fraser does, and he doesn't apologize for it. His fascination with popular culture has given him the kind of cultural literacy he needs to reach his audience – a kind of cultural literacy that is necessary to understand his plays.

But in an era when technology changes from year to year, and pop cult evolves and revolves from TV season to TV season, does Brad Fraser's use of pop cult idiom make *The Ugly Man* as transient as Betamax? After all, *The Changeling* still matters, 370-odd years after it was first performed. Will anyone care about *The Ugly Man* even 50 years from now?

Here's a last word from the playwright himself. "I don't think about being dated. I want audiences to come to see my plays now. Theatre is of the moment, it's live, it lives only in your memory. I want people in the theatre right here and right now. I don't care what happens after I'm dead."

Edmonton
April, 1993

First Performance

The Ugly Man, the winner of the 1989 Alberta Culture Playwriting Competition, was workshopped at Workshop West Theatre, Edmonton, in 1988 and 1989 and was presented as a Platform Play at Alberta Theatre Projects' playRites '90. It was given full production at playRites '92 under the direction of Bob White in the Martha Cohen Theatre, Calgary, running in repertory February 1-29.

Cast:

Sabina – *Claudia Blackwood*
Lottie – *Rae Ellen Bodie*
Forest – *Bruce McFee*
Veronica – *Lindsay Burns*
Acker – *Brian Stollery*
Leslie – *Jeffrey Hirschfield*
Cole – *Weston McMillan*

Set and Lighting – *Warren Carrie, Terry Gunvordahl*
Costume – *Gary Thorne*
Sound Design – *Allen Rae*
Dramaturg – *Charlotte Lee*
Producing Director – *D. Michael Dobbin*

The Ugly Man was next produced by Workshop West Theatre at the Kaasa Theatre, February 10, 1993, under the direction of Brad Fraser.

Cast:

Sabina – *Jill Dyck*
Lottie – *Kate Newby*
Forest – *Shaun Johnston*
Veronica – *Kate Ryan*
Acker – *Michael Spencer-Davis*
Leslie – *Jeffrey Hirschfield*
Cole – *Howard Kruschke*

Assistant Director – *Michael Clark*
Set and Costume Design – *David Skelton*
Composer/Sound Design – *Darrin Hagen*
Lighting – *Don McKenzie*

The Ugly Man is loosely adapted from *The Changeling* by Thomas Middleton and William Rowley.

Characters:

Forest, a man, 30s
Veronica, a woman, late teens
Sabina, a woman, late 40s
Acker, a man, 20s
Leslie, a man, 20s
Cole, a man, 20s
Lottie, a woman, 20s

Setting:

A well-appointed ranch-house and the attached garage.

SCENE 1

Sabina's office. Sabina is working. There is a knock at the door.

Sabina: Enter.

Lottie enters.

Lottie: Someone to see you, Miss Sabina.

Sabina: Who is it?

Lottie: Big fellow. Big ugly fellow.

Sabina: What does he want?

Lottie: Didn't say. He scared me, Ma'am.

Sabina: Why?

Lottie: The way he looks.

Sabina: How does he look, Lottie?

Lottie: Real bad.

Sabina: Send him in.

Lottie: Yes, Ma'am.

Lottie exits. Forest enters. Sabina stares at him for a long moment.

Sabina: Well.

Forest: My name is Forest.

Sabina: Yes?

Forest: I'm looking for work.

Sabina: What makes you think I'm hiring.

Forest: This is a big ranch. Big ranches need strong men.

Sabina: You on the lam?

Forest: No.

Sabina: Got a record?

Forest: No.

Sabina: Then why come all the way out here for a job?

Forest: I needed to get away.

Sabina: Someone break your heart?

Pause.

Forest: No.

Pause.

Sabina: All right. Throw your things in the bunkhouse with the other men. I'll start you in the field. Play your cards right, keep your nose clean and I might find something for you to do around the house.

Forest: I'm obliged.

Forest begins to exit.

Sabina: Forest?

Forest: Ma'am?

Sabina: Don't you want to know what I'm paying you?

Forest: No.

Forest exits.

SCENE 2

Veronica's bedroom. She is searching for something. After a moment she stamps her foot in frustration and calls out.

Veronica: Lottie?!

Lottie enters quickly.

Lottie: Yes, Miss Veronica?

Veronica: I can't find my stupid dress.

Lottie reaches into the closet and produces the dress.

Veronica: I looked in there.

Lottie: Sit down honey. You're all flushed.

Veronica: It's this damn heat.

Lottie: Miss Veronica, don't you use that blue language.

Veronica: Lottie, please.... I have a horrible headache.

Lottie: Poor baby. You want me to fix it?

Veronica: Yes.

Lottie moves onto the bed behind Veronica and softly touches Veronica's temples.

Veronica: Your hands are always so cool.

Lottie: Pain in the back or the front?

Veronica: Front.

Lottie passes the palms of her hands slowly across Veronica's forehead. Lottie sings softly.

Veronica: Ah!

Lottie: Be still.

Lottie moves forward and massages Veronica's hands.

Veronica: Ooh.

Lottie: Quiet.

Lottie taps each of Veronica's toes once.

Veronica: Oh.

Lottie: Now open your eyes.

Veronica: You're magical.

Lottie: I'll get a cold cloth for your forehead.

Veronica: This heat makes me so cross. I don't know why mother won't put air conditioning in this old place.

Sabina enters.

Sabina: Because, my darling, all they do is recycle polluted air and we'd constantly have the sniffles.

Veronica: But everyone has an air conditioner.

Sabina: Everyone might be jumping off the Brooklyn Bridge. That doesn't mean we would do it too. I'll have Lottie bring up a fan and a bowl of ice later. You can get that cloth, Lottie.

Lottie: Yes'm.

Lottie exits. Sabina picks up the dress on the bed and admires it.

Sabina: I always love this dress on you.

Veronica: I know.

Lottie enters with cloth.

Lottie: Here you are.

Sabina takes the cloth and lays it on Veronica's forehead.

Sabina: You may go, Lottie.

Lottie exits. Veronica takes the cloth from her head.

Veronica: I'm so tired of that dress.

Sabina: It's your colour.

Veronica: It's white. It's everybody's colour.

Sabina: Acker loves this dress.

Veronica: I want to wear green or yellow – or red.

Sabina: After you're married.

Veronica: Momma, everyone in the county knows I'm a virgin. I don't have to wear white to convince them.

Sabina: Sweetheart, you know how important it is to me that you wear white until you're married.

Veronica: Were you a virgin when you got married?

Short pause.

Sabina: I wish I had been.

Veronica: You weren't?

Sabina: No. I gave in to your father and let him think I was cheap and common. And he treated me accordingly.

Veronica: Daddy was bad.

Sabina: Men respect virgins. It shows strength of character.

Veronica: Did you and Daddy have good sex?

Sabina: Veronica!

Veronica: Momma, I'm nineteen.

Sabina: There were many things your father did not excel at. You needn't worry about it. Acker worships the ground you walk on.

Veronica: I know.

Sabina: He treats you with the respect you deserve.

Veronica: I know.

Sabina: He would never lie to you, or abuse you.

Veronica: I know!

Sabina: You're not having second thoughts are you?

Veronica: Little ones.

Sabina: Veronica, Acker's family is one of the oldest, richest and most respected in five counties. You've been crazy about each other since you were kids. All of a sudden you have doubts?

Veronica: Yes.

Sabina: Concentrate on the certain things, baby. It's the only way to get anywhere.

Veronica: Momma?...

Sabina: Hmm.

Veronica: Did you ever have good sex?

Sabina: You listen to me, young lady, the act of sexual intercourse is not the beautiful, meaningful thing the contraceptive companies want you to think it is. It's painful and it's messy and it leads to all sorts of complications.

Veronica: Some people have good sex.

Sabina: Certainly. Men. Now lie down and rest your eyes. Acker and his groomsmen will be here soon.

Sabina kisses Veronica on the forehead and exits.

SCENE 3

The drawing-room. Acker, Leslie and Cole are there sipping aperitifs.

Leslie: So the one guy says to the other one, we might as well. The room's paid for.

Short pause. No one laughs. Acker gives Leslie an affectionate squeeze.

Acker: Leslie, it's damn good to have you back.

Leslie: It's good to see you.

Acker: And Cole, I can't believe it's been so long. You look great.

Leslie: I've taken good care of him.

Cole: When do we get to meet the blushing bride?

Acker: She's getting ready, so within the next hour – or two.

Leslie: Is she still the prettiest girl in the county?

Acker: I'd be lying if I said no.

Cole: Sounds interesting.

Leslie: Watch out, Acker. Cole bats those baby blues at someone and they're flat on their back with their legs in the air like that. *Snaps his fingers.*

Acker: You don't know my Veronica.

Cole: She sounds very special.

Acker: There isn't another like her.

Sabina enters dressed for dinner.

Sabina: Gentlemen.

Acker: Miss Sabina. You remember my brother Leslie.

Sabina: Of course – Leslie. How nice to see you after so many years.

Leslie: You haven't changed a bit.

Sabina: You're lying of course, but I do appreciate it. I like the moustache. It covers the scar quite nicely and gives your appearance a certain dash.

Leslie: Thank you very much.

Sabina: I'm glad to see you're not self-conscious about it. Tell me Acker, what is it about a man with a cleft palate that makes his eyes so vulnerable?

Acker: I'm sure I wouldn't know.

Sabina: It's an observation, not an insult, Acker. I find your younger brother most charming.

Acker: You remember Cole.

Sabina: The best man. Of course.

Cole: That was a long time ago.

Sabina: Not to someone my age. You've developed well.

Cole: Thank you.

Sabina: I see Lottie's taken care of your drinks. I think I'll have a scotch.

Leslie: Allow me.

Sabina: I'd practically insist. The Glenfiddich please. You boys all look so nice tonight.

Leslie hands her the drink. Sabina raises her glass in a toast.

Sabina: To the groomsmen who have come such a long way.

Acker: Here here.

They drink.

Cole: I'd forgotten how beautiful your ranch is.

Sabina: Thank you, Cole. I hope you won't find the west too hot.

Cole: No ma'am. It gets hot in the east too.

Sabina: I know. But it's so much wetter there.

Cole: I like the humidity actually.

Sabina: I thought so. You have that look about you.

Lottie enters.

Lottie: Miss Veronica.

Veronica enters. The men greet her simultaneously.

Acker: Darling...

Cole: Well well...

Leslie: Veronica...

left to right – Michael Spencer-Davis as Acker, Jeffrey Hirschfield as Leslie, Jill Dyck as Sabina, and Howard Kruschke as Cole.

Veronica moves to Acker and kisses him on the cheek.

Veronica: Darling. Leslie, good to see you.

Leslie: You look great.

Acker: Veronica, do you remember Cole?

Veronica looks at Cole. Pause.

Veronica: Not really.

Cole: Hello.

Short pause.

Acker: *To Veronica.* Darling, are you okay?

Veronica: Yes. Sure. I'm just a little... warm.

Acker: Cole used to come out summers.

Cole: Our fathers were friends.

Acker: We didn't hang out around here much.

Leslie: We weren't very interested in girls – then.

Sabina: Shall we eat?

Acker: Please.

Sabina: Hattie really has outdone herself tonight.

Forest enters suddenly, very out of breath. His shirt is torn and his hands are covered in blood.

Forest: We've got a problem!

Veronica gasps. She is looking at Forest's face, not the blood.

Acker: My God!

Sabina: Forest, what's happened?!

Forest: Accident. In the breeding pens.

Sabina: What?

Forest: Young Washington was gored by one of the bulls. I've tied the artery off but he's got to get to a hospital.

Sabina: Acker, have Sam get the car ready. Lottie, get this man a towel. Leslie, see if he's hurt.

Acker and Lottie exit.

Forest: I'm fine.

Sabina: Do as you're told. Leslie, pour him a shot of whiskey.

All exit but Forest, Leslie, and Veronica. Leslie pours Forest a drink.

Leslie: You cut?

Forest: No.

Leslie: Take your shirt off. I'll check.

Lottie enters with a towel. Forest removes his shirt.

Lottie: Here you go.

Leslie takes the towel from Lottie and wipes blood from Forest.

Leslie: Thanks.

Lottie: I'll get him one of Sam's old shirts.

Lottie exits. Leslie wipes the last of the blood away.

Leslie: You're in good shape.

Forest: Thanks.

Leslie: No cuts.

Forest: Something wrong Miss?

Veronica: I – I never could stand the sight of blood.

Forest: It's all been wiped off.

Acker enters.

Acker: Sam'll have that boy at the hospital in minutes. You handled that very well.

Forest: Thanks.

Acker: *Extending his hand.* Acker Groveland. My brother Leslie.

Forest shakes hands with them.

Forest: Thanks for cleaning me up.

Leslie: My pleasure.

Acker: And, of course, my fiancée, Veronica.

Forest: Hello.

Veronica gives him a quick smile, still not looking at him.

Acker: You're one of the new men.

Forest: Yes.

Acker: Glad to have you aboard.

Forest: I should go.

Acker: Nonsense, have another drink.

Leslie: Yeah.

Leslie goes to the bar and pours Forest another drink.

Acker: You've got the look of the military about you.

Forest: Sweden. Four years.

Leslie: Wow.

Acker: Tell me, Washington wasn't teasing that animal was he?

Forest: No. I was showing him how to help the bull.

Leslie: Help it?

Forest: Into the cow. Sometimes the male has problems.

Acker: Problems?

Forest: Entering the cow.

Acker: Of course. We have horses. Leslie, let's go see what's keeping the others.

Leslie: Sure.

Acker: Forest, would you mind staying with Veronica until we get back?

Forest: Not a bit.

Acker and Leslie exit.

Veronica: I'm quite all right on my own.

Forest: Of course I'll go.

Sabina and Cole enter.

Sabina: You'll do no such thing.

Veronica: Acker and Leslie just went to find you.

Forest: How is he?

Sabina: He'll live. The bull, however, will be shot.

Forest: No point.

Sabina: It's dangerous.

Forest: The bull thought Washington and I were interfering with a delicate process.

Sabina: Are you willing to accept responsibility if it hurts someone else?

Forest: Sure.

Sabina: Good for you.

Acker and Leslie enter.

Leslie: Where were you guys?

Cole: The holding pens.

Veronica: Acker, what's wrong with you?

Leslie: He's okay.

Acker: My very considerate brother is attempting to save me the embarrassment of revealing that the sight of all of that blood made me quite ill.

Cole: Good old Acker.

Leslie: He's never liked the sight of blood.

Sabina: Acker was meant for other things.

Acker: Like dinner.

Sabina: Forest, do come see me in my office first thing tomorrow.

Forest: Sure.

Sabina: Come children, let's see if we can salvage some of Hattie's handiwork.

Leslie: Good meeting you.

Forest: Good night, Miss.

Veronica: Good night.

Forest exits.

Acker: What an amazing fellow.

Cole: What an amazing face.

Veronica: He's horrible.

Sabina: Now children, looks aren't everything.

Cole: They help.

Sabina: That man's got potential.

Veronica: Mother. Please.

Sabina: Come.

All exit but Veronica and Cole. They stare at one another.

Cole: Nice place. Big.

Veronica: Yes.

Cole takes a step toward Veronica.

Cole: I think you're –

Veronica cuts him off quickly.

Veronica: Not now.

Cole: When?

Veronica: Soon.

Leslie enters. Pause.

Leslie: Dinner.

Veronica: Yes.

Veronica exits quickly.

Leslie: Dinner.

Cole: Yes.

They exit.

SCENE 4

Sabina's office. Morning. Sabina is working at her desk.
There is a knock at the door.

Sabina: Enter.

Forest enters.

Sabina: Acker tells me you fought in Sweden.

Forest: That's right.

Sabina: What do you know about me?

Forest: That you'll hire a man, no questions asked, pay him
fairly, and let him leave whenever he likes.

Sabina: What else?

Forest: Your husband made a fortune running drugs over the
border. He was ruthless and dangerous. He was shot to
death in an alley seven years ago and his only legal asset
was this ranch, which you've managed to turn into a
money-making proposition in a short length of time.

Sabina: You impress me.

Forest: It's not intentional.

Sabina: Why are you here?

Forest: Here's as good as anywhere.

Sabina: I want to give you a promotion.

Forest: Why?

Sabina: I need a body guard. It's for my daughter.

Forest: What's the problem?

Sabina: She's not... experienced. I've protected her for as
long as I can, but – well – there are certain things that

can only be kept in check for so long. She's a virgin, Forest, and – well, she's starting to get curious. I'm afraid she might be tempted to make some... dangerous decisions.

Forest: Don't you trust her?

Sabina: We all make mistakes.

Forest: I could keep an eye on her.

Sabina: As far as anyone else is concerned you're the new chauffeur. I'll have Sam install you in the driver's suite above the garage.

Forest begins to exit.

Sabina: Forest?

Forest: Yes?

Sabina: Your face – was there an accident, or were you born like that.

Forest: I'll answer that question for you if you'll answer one for me.

Sabina: That's fair.

Forest: Why do you think it's so important that your daughter be a virgin?

Sabina: Because I believe that if a woman gives herself to a man without making him wait, that man will never respect or truly love her. I believe that there is a power in virginity and a woman must choose very carefully where and when she uses that power.

Forest: Do you speak from experience?

Sabina: One question. Now, your face, was it an accident or were you born like that?

Forest: Yes.

Forest exits. Sabina smiles and nods.

SCENE 5

*The veranda. Evening. Acker enters and knocks at the door.
Lottie answers it.*

Acker: Hello Lottie, how are you today?

Lottie: I can't complain. Is Mr. Cole with you?

Acker: He was dawdling so I left him behind. He'll catch up
soon enough.

Lottie: Oh good.

Acker: Why Lottie, I believe you might be developing a
crush on our Cole.

Lottie: Mr. Acker! Go on!

Acker: Are you blushing?

Veronica enters.

Acker: You become more radiant every day.

Veronica: I feel good. Where's Cole?

Acker: Don't tell me that handsome rogue's turned your
head too.

Veronica: *Kisses him quickly.* Silly. A bride should get to
know her husband's best man.

Acker: Are you excited, Darling?

Veronica: *Moving away from him.* Yes. Very.

Lottie: Would you like some fresh lemonade, Mr. Acker?

Acker: I would love one, thank you.

Veronica: Me too. Lots of ice.

Lottie exits. Acker puts his arms around Veronica.

Acker: This heat.

Veronica: The summer would be so perfect if it would cool off a bit.

Forest enters and watches Acker and Veronica. They do not notice him. Forest is now dressed in driver's livery.

Acker: Brilliant sunset.

Veronica: Mmm.

Acker: I hope Cole sees it.

Veronica: Oh Acker, you should go find him.

Acker: He'll be along.

Veronica: He should share this with us.

Forest: I'll go.

Veronica: How long have you been there?

Forest: Just a minute.

Veronica: Well you should – should cough or clear your throat or something. It's not polite to stand and watch people.

Forest: I apologize.

Acker: Not to worry. It's rather handy, really. Now I can stay here with Veronica. Right?

Veronica: Right.

Lottie enters with lemonades.

Lottie: Oh – would you like a lemonade too, Mr. Forest?

Forest: No thanks.

Cole enters carrying an armful of flowers.

Cole: Sorry. I saw a field full of these beauties and they made me think of the lovely ladies at this house. I couldn't resist picking an armful.

Acker: What a wonderful thought.

Veronica: Yes.

Cole hands a small bunch of the flowers to Lottie.

Cole: For you, Gorgeous.

Lottie: Mr. Cole! Thank you!

Cole hands Lottie another bunch of flowers.

Cole: For Miss Sabina.

Lottie: She'll love them.

Cole hands the rest of the flowers to Veronica.

Cole: And, for The Bride.

Veronica: Thank you. They're beautiful. And you're just in time to enjoy this wonderful sunset with us. *Hands flowers to Lottie.* Put these in water and a bit of ginger ale.

Lottie exits.

Acker: Cole, you're amazing. I never think of things like that.

Veronica: Just look how red the clouds have turned.

Cole: Beautiful.

Acker: Yes.

Veronica: Forest, isn't there something you should be doing?

Forest: Of course.

Acker: Oh Forest, the engine of my car has developed a bit of a knock. Will you have a look at it tomorrow?

Forest: Bring it by.

Forest exits.

Acker: Veronica, that was rude.

Veronica: He gives me the creeps.

Cole: He doesn't say much.

Veronica: He's always looking at me. Spying.

Acker: Why would he be spying on you?

Veronica: He was spying on me just now.

Acker: Darling, he was watching the sunset, just like the rest of us.

Veronica: There's something – something wrong with him.

Cole: Sure is ugly.

Acker: We're missing the sunset.

Cole: Yes.

Veronica: Come here, both of you.

They go to her, standing on either side. She puts an arm around each of them. All stare at the sunset.

Cole: Now there's something we don't see out east.

Acker: I do hope it's like this, always.

Veronica: Yes.

Cole: Yes.

Veronica and Cole look at one another as Acker continues to stare off into the sunset. Veronica silently mouths "tonight" to Cole.

SCENE 6

The garage. Night. Forest is working on some engine parts with an acetylene torch. After he has mended them he cleans them. Leslie enters.

Leslie: Still working on that Packard?

Forest: Yes.

Leslie: Give you a hand?

Forest: If you want.

Leslie: I'm tired of wedding plans.

Forest: I'm told it's a special time.

Leslie: Think you'll ever get that old thing running?

Forest: It keeps me busy.

Leslie: Veronica's dad used to be so proud of that car.

Forest: They don't make them like this anymore.

Leslie: Nope.

Pause.

Leslie: Where you from?

Forest: Oh – all over.

Pause.

Leslie: You mind if I ask you something?

Forest: About my face?

Leslie: You ever thought about plastic surgery?

Forest: When I was younger.

Leslie: Never tried it?

Forest: Costs a lot. And with my face they can't make any guarantees.

Leslie: I've thought about it.

Forest: Yeah?

Leslie: What do you think?

Forest: I think – sometimes – changing our faces for other people doesn't change them for ourselves.

Pause.

Forest: There are advantages to being ugly, Les.

Leslie: *Laughs nervously.* No one ever calls me Les.

Forest: You mind?

Leslie: Naw.

Forest: Good.

Leslie: When you're – you know – not beautiful – people treat you different. They always say things like you're so good at this or you're so good at that – or you're so nice. I hate being called nice.

Forest: You're an attractive boy, Les.

Leslie: You should see me without the moustache.

Pause. They clean. Forest is cleaning a length of pipe.

Leslie: You queer?

Forest: No.

Leslie: You're not into guys?

Forest: I didn't say that.

Leslie: I like guys better.

Forest: I like beautiful things that make me feel good.

Leslie: Like Cole.

Forest: Too pretty.

Leslie: He's beautiful.

Forest: You love him?

Leslie: We – uh – we usta do stuff. When we were kids. And at school. He taught me stuff.

Forest: Yeah?

Leslie: He doesn't want me to do them so much anymore.

Forest: Ah.

Leslie: I'll be so glad when this stupid wedding's over. Then we can go back east and everything'll be all right.

Forest: You won't have to wait too long.

Leslie: I should get back. They're probably ready to go.

Forest: Sure.

Pause.

Leslie: You mind if I come by again sometime?

Forest: No.

Leslie: Great.

Leslie exits. Forest continues to clean the pipe with long, slow strokes even though it is now quite shiny. He smiles to himself.

SCENE 7

The veranda. Night. Veronica and Acker are on the steps.

Acker: I thought Cole was never going to leave. We never seem to be alone anymore.

Veronica: We will be. *Short pause.* Soon.

Pause.

Acker: I'd like a kiss.

Veronica gives him a peck on the lips.

Acker: A real kiss.

Veronica: Honey, it's so hot.

Acker: Please.

Veronica kisses him. He grabs her, pulls her closer, and kisses her passionately. She pulls away.

Acker: Ronnie?

Veronica: Nothing. I'm just – just nervous.

Acker: I can't imagine life without you.

Veronica: *Not looking at him.* I know exactly how you feel.

Pause.

Acker: Look at the meadow. All that moonlight. *He begins to touch Veronica amorously.* The long grass waving. The shadow of the forest. You know, we could take a walk out there. Just the two of us. Sit by the stream. Lie down under the stars. Be alone.

Acker now has his hand on her breast. Pause. Veronica pulls away from him gently. Acker puts his hand in his pocket.

Veronica: It's late.

Acker: Yes.

Acker gets on his knees before Veronica and takes her hands.

Acker: I'd never do anything to hurt you.

Veronica: Of course you wouldn't.

Veronica exits. Acker stands, staring at the moon for a moment.

SCENE 8

Sabina's office. Sabina is working at her desk. It is night. Veronica enters without knocking.

Veronica: You should be in bed.

Sabina: I've got to balance these ledgers by morning. Why are you still up?

Veronica: Not tired.

Sabina: I hope you haven't inherited my insomnia.

Veronica: Momma, are you having that horrible man watch me?

Sabina: I like Forest.

Veronica: Don't avoid the question.

Sabina: I have asked him to keep an eye on you.

Veronica: Why?

Sabina: Because you are my only child and I love you.

Veronica: I don't like him.

Sabina: Let's go to the kitchen and have a cup of tea.

Veronica: I don't want any tea.

Sabina: But we communicate so much better in the kitchen.

Veronica: Momma, he scares me.

Sabina: You know I would never let anything that could harm you within a hundred miles of this place.

Veronica: I hate him!

Sabina: Stop this.

Veronica: He's ugly and he's evil!

Sabina: This is not how I raised you young lady. You know better than to judge someone solely on how they look.

Veronica: But I don't like him!

Sabina: Veronica, you're going to be married and living on Acker's ranch. I'll be alone. And when I am I want someone around here who'll look out for me. I think Forest may be that man.

Veronica: It's a mistake.

Sabina: Girl, you've got a lot more to worry about right now than who I hire to work for me. Now get yourself off to bed.

Veronica: Aren't you tired?

Sabina: I wish I were.

Veronica: I'll get your pills.

Sabina: They always make me dopey in the morning.

Veronica: You know how cranky you get when you haven't had a good night's sleep.

Sabina: This is true.

Veronica: I'm not the only one who has a lot on their mind right now.

Sabina: You're right.

Veronica: Of course I am. Now come on. I'll get you a glass of water and tuck you in.

Sabina: Veronica, you're a good daughter.

Veronica: I know.

They exit.

SCENE 9

Veronica's room. Lottie is dozing in a chair. A shadowed figure appears in the window, looking into the room. Seeing Lottie, it withdraws. Lottie awakens with a snort and looks around, momentarily disoriented. She walks to the window and looks out. Veronica enters.

Veronica: Lottie!

Lottie jumps, startled.

Veronica: What are you doing?

Lottie: Stayed up to see if you needed anything.

Veronica: I'm sorry Lottie. I should've told you I'd be up for a while tonight. Go to bed this instant.

Lottie: Yes'm.

Lottie exits. Veronica closes the door after Lottie and locks it. There is a quiet knock on her window. She opens the window and Cole clambers in.

Veronica: Did Lottie see you?

Cole: She was sound asleep.

Cole grabs her and kisses her passionately. She returns the kiss with equal enthusiasm.

Veronica: You're so beautiful.

Cole: You can't marry him.

Veronica: I have to.

She grabs him and kisses him ferociously.

Cole: From the minute I saw you I knew.

Veronica: Yes!

Cole: Acker's not the one for you.

Veronica: Don't.

Cole: You'll be wasted with him.

They sit on the bed.

Veronica: He loves me so much.

Cole: He'll get over it.

Veronica: Mother would die of disappointment.

Cole: She won't.

Much kissing etc. throughout this.

Veronica: It's gone too far. I could never get out of it.

Cole: But I love you!

Veronica: Don't say that!

Cole: You have no idea. The things I've done. I've always said there's no such thing as love. That I didn't want it to happen to me. But the second I laid eyes on you I knew I was wrong. You can't marry him!

Veronica: I have to!

Cole: Why?

Veronica: Because – because he loves me. Because he's from the right family. Because I *have* to. It's just the way things are.

Cole: I don't believe this.

Veronica: Acker would die. And so would Mother.

Cole: She wants you to be happy.

Veronica: But this will make me happy. Acker is very nice. He treats me well. He has a lot of money.

Cole moves away from Veronica. Veronica goes to Cole and touches him.

Veronica: Marrying Acker doesn't mean we can't be friends.

Cole embraces Veronica lustily.

Veronica: But not yet.

Veronica pulls away from Cole.

Cole: What?

Veronica: Cole, a great deal has been made out of my being a virgin. Mother tells everyone. And Acker – I've been putting him off for years. If I'm not a virgin the night I marry, he'll know. Everyone will know.

Cole: I have to have you.

Veronica: You'd make me a hypocrite.

Cole: I'd make you a very happy woman.

Veronica: I can't. *Short pause.* I want to be a virgin when I get married. I'll do anything else you want. Dirty things. Filthy things.

Cole: Veronica, the only thing I haven't done is have a virgin.

Veronica: Please understand. *She sinks to her knees.* I'll do anything else.

Cole: *Pulling her up.* Everyone's done that.

Veronica: After the wedding. Anything.

Cole: I can't wait that long!

Veronica: I love you, Cole.

Cole: Then marry me.

Veronica: It's too late.

Cole: You've got to choose.

Veronica: But I hardly know you.

Cole: It doesn't matter. We were made for each other. You know it as well as I do.

Veronica: I can't!

Cole: Then I can't stay here!

Veronica: No, wait!

Cole: I love you, Veronica. But I can't share you. Goodbye.

Cole exits. Veronica closes the window.

SCENE 10

The drawing room. Day. Sabina enters with a basket of freshly cut red roses. She begins to arrange them in a vase. Lottie enters.

Sabina: Is Veronica still sleeping?

Lottie: Yes'm. She's got her door locked.

Sabina: Locked? How unusual.

Acker and Leslie enter.

Acker: Good morning.

Sabina: Gentlemen. You're looking fit this morning. Well, you are, Acker. Leslie, did you not sleep well?

Leslie: A bit of insomnia.

Acker: Beautiful roses, Miss Sabina.

Sabina: They only bloom for two weeks I'm afraid. Where's your other partner in crime?

Leslie: Didn't come home last night.

Acker: Knowing Cole he probably spent the night in town, threatening the virtue of every waitress he met.

Leslie: I didn't hear him go out.

Forest enters. The others don't notice him.

Sabina: Perhaps he's found wedding preparations tedious?

Leslie: Perhaps.

Forest: Where's Veronica?

Sabina: Sound asleep, Forest. You needn't worry.

Acker: I was hoping she'd have brunch with us.

Sabina: She'll be up soon. Lottie, have Hattie make some tea.

Lottie: Yes'm.

Lottie exits.

Sabina: This heat. We are long overdue for a bit of rain.

Acker: It'll break eventually.

Veronica enters.

Sabina: About time, Sleepyhead.

Acker: *Going to her.* Good morning, Darling.

Veronica: *Waving him away.* Morning.

Sabina: Someone's grumpy.

Veronica: Where's Cole?

Acker: Who knows? Anyway, we're here. Would you like to brunch with us?

Veronica: No.

Lottie enters with a tray of tea.

Lottie: Tea.

Lottie serves tea to all.

Sabina: Veronica, we absolutely must choose our boutonnières today. We can't put it off another minute.

Veronica: All right, all right.

Sabina: Forest, prepare for a trip into town.

Forest: Sure.

Veronica: Would everyone please stop staring at me?!

Pause.

Sabina: No one's staring at you, Darling.

Acker: Ronnie, is something wrong?

Veronica: Oh! Just leave me alone!

Sabina: Nerves.

Veronica: It is *not* nerves!

Pause. All stare at her.

Veronica: I – I'm feeling a little crampy.

Lottie: Too long in bed.

Sabina: Lottie, tell Hattie to whip up something brunchy. We'll eat here.

Lottie: Yes'm.

Lottie exits.

Sabina: Honey, do you want to lie down?

Veronica: I'll be fine.

Acker: I understand.

Veronica: Of course you do.

Sabina: Veronica, did you have trouble sleeping last night?

Veronica: *Referring to Forest.* Would someone tell him to stop staring at me!

Acker: Ronnie?!

Forest: Forgive me.

Forest exits. Lottie enters.

Lottie: Eggs are on.

Veronica: I think I will go lie down after all.

Veronica exits.

Sabina: Acker? Leslie?

Leslie: I'm not that hungry anymore.

Leslie exits.

Acker: Everyone certainly is on edge this morning.

Sabina: Yes.

Acker: Must be the excitement.

Sabina: Must be.

They exit.

SCENE 11

The veranda. Veronica sits in the shade fanning herself. Forest enters from the house. He does not see Veronica.

Veronica: Can I help you?

Forest: I didn't realize you were here.

Forest begins to exit.

Veronica: No. Wait.

Forest stops.

Veronica: I – I'm sorry.

Forest: Is it my face that offends you so much?

Veronica: No.

Forest: Then why can't you look at me?

Veronica: Mother likes you a great deal.

Forest: She's a generous woman.

Veronica: You don't say much.

Forest: I admire economy.

Veronica: Where are you from?

Forest: All over.

Veronica: I've never gone anywhere.

Forest: You're well taken care of here.

Veronica: I want to go to places like Europe or Africa or Russia. I'd like to see history. Great works of art. That kind of stuff.

Forest: I've spent time in Europe.

Veronica: Have you seen any great works of art?

Forest: I saw Michelangelo's *David*.

Veronica: And?...

Forest: I have things I should be doing.

Forest starts to exit.

Veronica: Wait.

Forest stops.

Veronica: How long were you in the army?

Forest: Four years.

Veronica: You ever... kill anyone?

Pause.

Forest: Have you ever killed anyone?

Veronica: Me? Don't be silly. I could never...

Forest: I don't make assumptions.

Pause.

Veronica: Have you ever had a girlfriend or anything?

Forest: I've had women.

Veronica: What sorts of women?

Forest: All sorts.

Veronica: I bet you've had a fascinating life.

Forest: Yes.

Sabina enters.

Sabina: Veronica, you're not actually talking to Forest are you?

Veronica: Mo-ther.

Sabina: Have you decided he might be worth knowing – or do you want something?

Veronica: What do you think?

Sabina: Forest, we're a bit short of vermouth and dubonnet. Would you mind?

Forest: Of course not.

Forest exits.

Veronica: I bet he could be real dangerous.

Sabina: Couldn't everyone?

Veronica: It's hot.

SCENE 12

The drawing room. Lottie is serving coffee to Acker and Leslie. There is a knock at the door and Cole enters.

Lottie: Mr. Cole!

Leslie: You look like shit.

Cole: Thank you.

Leslie: Where were you?

Cole: Out.

Leslie: Right.

Acker: I knew being in the country would get to you eventually.

Lottie: Coffee, Mr. Cole?

Cole: No.

Lottie exits.

Cole: I need a drink.

Acker: So early?

Cole: Yes.

Acker: I could get a scotch from Miss Sabina's liquor cabinet.

Cole: Good.

Acker exits.

Leslie: Well?...

Cole: Leslie, don't play the jilted lover right now.

Leslie goes to Cole and embraces him around the waist.

Leslie: I'm sorry.

Cole: Don't be.

Acker enters. Seeing Leslie and Cole he clears his throat in embarrassment. They break the embrace guiltily. Short pause.

Acker: One scotch.

Cole: Thanks.

Cole downs the entire drink.

Acker: So, have you had some great adventure?

Cole: Sure.

Veronica, Sabina, and Lottie enter.

Sabina: You did strike me as the adventurous type, Cole. Are you hung over or upset?

Cole: Hello, Veronica.

Sabina: I'm afraid you've missed brunch.

Cole: I just came by to tell you all that I'm leaving.

Leslie: What?

Acker: Leaving?

Veronica: You can't!

Lottie: No.

All stare at Lottie for a moment. She looks away, embarrassed.

Cole: Tonight. I've already booked a flight. Something's come up in the east. It can't wait.

Acker: But Cole, I don't understand...

Cole: This is very important.

Acker: More important than my wedding?

Cole: Yes.

Pause.

Sabina: If Cole feels that strongly about it there's really nothing we can do. Leslie can take his place.

Acker: It won't be the same.

Leslie: No.

Sabina: We'll just have to get by. Now, let's not drag the farewells out.

Cole: I have to go into town and send a wire home. I'll just stay there until my plane's ready to go.

Sabina: Forest will drive you in.

Cole: I have a rental.

Sabina: How convenient.

Cole: Have a wonderful wedding.

Leslie: I'll go back to the ranch with you.

Cole: No.

Cole begins to exit.

Veronica: Cole?

Cole: Yes?

Veronica: Aren't you going to kiss the bride?

Acker: It really would be bad luck if you didn't.

Cole: Yes.

Slowly Cole moves to Veronica. He kisses her lightly on the lips. He moves to exit.

Cole: Goodbye.

Cole exits.

Lottie: Goodbye, Mr. Cole.

All stare at Lottie.

Lottie: Goodbye, Miss Sabina. Goodbye, Mr. Acker.

Lottie exits.

Acker: I hope he's not in some sort of trouble.

Sabina: He seems most adept at avoiding it.

Veronica: I wish everyone would stop talking so much!

Veronica exits quickly.

Leslie: Excuse me.

Leslie exits.

Acker: Everyone sure is –

Sabina: *Cutting him off.* It's the heat.

SCENE 13

The garage. Night. Forest has his shirt off and is assembling engine parts. He is drinking a can of beer. Veronica enters.

Veronica: It smells like oil in here.

Forest: It is a garage.

Veronica: Right.

Forest: Beer?

Veronica: All right.

Forest gets Veronica a beer and opens it for her.

Veronica: Have you got a glass? Probably not, right?

Forest: Right.

Pause.

Forest: What can I do for you?

Veronica: I want to – to apologize, for the way I've been
treating you.

Forest: Don't.

Veronica: Don't what?

Forest: Don't be nice to me.

Veronica: Why not?

Forest: It's not necessary.

Veronica: But I want to.

Pause.

Forest: Do you any idea how beautiful you are?

Veronica: Yes.

Forest: I can smell you. Over the dust and the oil and the beer I can still smell you. Shampoo. Soap. Lemon. A bit of sweat. Your skin.

Veronica: Do you... like that smell?

Forest: Be careful.

Pause.

Veronica: We could be friends.

Forest: Only as long as you want something from me.

Veronica: Aren't all relationships like that?

Forest: What do you want?

Veronica: Cole is leaving.

Forest: I heard.

Veronica: I have to see him.

Forest: Why?

Veronica: I love him.

Forest: I thought you loved Acker.

Veronica: It's different with Acker.

Forest: Different how?

Veronica: Will you help me or not?

Forest: Why don't you just go get Cole yourself?

Veronica: He's in town already. And I think Mother suspects.

Forest: Suspects what?

Veronica: Quit acting so dense.

Forest: What's in it for me?

Veronica: My gratitude. My friendship.

Forest: Lucky me.

Veronica: Do it for the way I smell.

Forest: Be careful Veronica.

Veronica: Please.

Forest: Your mother trusted me to keep these things from happening.

Veronica: Forget her. I have to see Cole!

Veronica moves to him, steels herself, and lays one of her hands on his shoulder. He pulls away.

Forest: I'm ugly, not stupid.

Veronica: I'll make it worth your while.

Pause.

Forest: I'll need your mother's permission to use the car.

Veronica: Take my Jag. Don't turn the lights on until you're out of the driveway. Hurry. He'll be at the airport by now.

Forest exits.

Sabina's office. Night. There is a knock at the door.

Sabina: Enter.

Lottie enters.

Lottie: You wanted to see me, Ma'am?

Sabina: Close the door.

Lottie closes the door.

Lottie: Everyone sure is in a state today.

Sabina: Yes.

Lottie: Means the weather's gonna change.

Sabina: Lottie, I miss your mother.

Lottie: God rest her soul.

Sabina: She was more than a maid, Lottie. She was my friend.

Lottie: She always spoke well of you, Miss Sabina.

Sabina: Can I tell you something, Lottie? Something I've never told anyone before?

Lottie: I guess so.

Sabina: Some years ago, when my husband was alive – after Veronica was born – I found out I was pregnant again. I couldn't stand the thought of bearing another of that man's children. Especially if it turned out to be a boy. I knew a boy would have to grow up to be just like his father. So your mother gave me something, Lottie. A potion that made the baby go away.

Lottie: Miss Sabina, you're not pregnant are you?

Sabina: Of course not. What I'm getting at is – I know your mother had certain – let's say talents. Did she pass any of those things on to you?

Lottie: Some.

Sabina: Do you know of any way to find out whether or not someone is a virgin?

Lottie: Yes'm.

Sabina: I thought you might.

Lottie: We'll need certain things.

Sabina: Make a list.

Lottie begins to write down a list. There is a knock at the door.

Sabina: Not a word. Enter.

Forest enters.

Forest: Just checking to see if you needed anything before I turned in.

Sabina: No. Thank you for checking.

Forest: Good night.

Forest exits. Lottie is finished writing the list. She hands it to Sabina, who scans it quickly.

Sabina: The heart of a vulture?

Lottie: We might be able to use a chicken.

Sabina: Fabulous.

Sabina and Lottie exit.

SCENE 15

The garage. Night. Forest and Cole enter. Cole carries his suitcase.

Cole: I hope you realize that flight didn't have cancellation insurance.

Forest: I checked with the agent. You didn't even have a reservation.

Cole: Maybe I was going stand-by.

Veronica enters.

Veronica: I knew you'd come.

Cole: Why can't you let me go?

Veronica: Because I can't. Forest, could you leave us alone?

Forest: If you like.

Veronica: Wait.

Forest turns. She goes to him and takes his hand. She doesn't look at his face.

Veronica: Thank you.

Forest: It wasn't a favour, Veronica.

Pause.

Forest: I'll leave you two alone.

Forest disappears into the shadows of the garage.

Cole: This isn't right.

Veronica: I don't know what's right, I only know what I want.

There is the muffled, distant sound of thunder.

Cole: I can't stay here knowing you'll be with him!

Veronica: Just once, Cole. Once!

Cole: It's got to be him or me. If you don't choose, I will be on the next plane, and no one will bring me back.

A peal of thunder, slightly louder.

Veronica: You don't understand!

Cole: I do understand!

Cole grabs Veronica and kisses her. It grows very passionate. There is a loud, immediate clap of thunder. The garage door opens. Acker is standing there.

Acker: Forest, have you?...

Acker stares at Veronica and Cole in horror.

Cole: Acker!

Veronica: Damn!

There is another clap of thunder and a flash of lightning.

Veronica: You don't understand.

Acker: *Takes a few stumbling steps into the room.* I'm sorry – I – I – forgive me!

Acker turns and suddenly runs from the garage.

Veronica: He knows!

Cole: Acker!

Veronica: Cole! No!

Cole exits quickly. Veronica moves to the door and looks out. The storm subsides slightly. Veronica turns and looks into the darkness.

Veronica: You've been there the whole time, haven't you?

Forest: *From the darkness.* Yes.

Veronica: Are you laughing at me?

Forest: Only inside.

Veronica: It's not easy you know. One's got everything and the other one's gorgeous.

Forest: Quite a predicament.

Veronica: You don't understand. You're not like us.

Forest: No.

Veronica: Acker is very upset. He could get into trouble out there. He's in those woods. He could do anything.

Forest: Yes.

Veronica: Hurt himself. Fall down. Trip.

Forest: Yes.

Veronica: Those woods go on for miles.

Pause.

Veronica: They might not find him for years. If at all.

Forest is now at the edge of the light.

Forest: I can smell you.

Veronica: You're experienced at this sort of thing.

Forest moves into the light, behind Veronica, and puts his arms around her. She stiffens but doesn't move.

Forest: It's murder.

Veronica: I know.

Forest: What will you give me?

Veronica: Money. Lots of money.

Forest: I don't need money.

There is a clap of thunder.

Veronica: Find him.

Forest: You owe me.

Veronica: Yes.

Forest: Anything.

Veronica: Just make sure he never comes back!

A louder clap of thunder. Forest exits.

SCENE 16

The drawing-room. Night. Lottie holds a steaming vial in her hand. She and Sabina stare at it.

Lottie: Just slip it into some drink and you'll know right away whether the lady is a virgin or not.

Lottie corks the vial. Sabina takes it from her and conceals it in her clothing.

Sabina: What's the reaction?

Lottie: If she's pure – nothing.

Sabina: And if she's not?

Lottie: Craziness, Miss. Big craziness.

Sabina: Lottie, thank you. There'll be a little something extra in your pay envelope this week.

Veronica enters, dripping with rain.

Sabina: Ronnie?!

Veronica: Momma, it's horrible – horrible!

Sabina: What are you talking about?

Veronica: Acker – he's run off into the forest.

Sabina: Why?

Veronica: He – he came into the garage. I was saying – saying goodbye to Cole.

Sabina: Cole left hours ago.

Veronica: He came back.

Sabina: You little fool!

Veronica: I had to Momma. My heart...

Sabina: *Cutting her off.* Hearts are for weaklings, Veronica. Hearts make women do stupid things.

Veronica: I'm so worried.

Sabina: Do you love Cole?

Veronica: I don't know.

Sabina: You've jeopardized your entire future for someone you don't love?

Veronica: I don't love Acker either.

Sabina: You're marrying him. It's not important that you love him.

Veronica: I wanted Cole.

Sabina: Then you should've waited until after you were married and taken him as your lover.

Veronica: Momma!

Sabina: Acker's romantic, but he's hardly passionate.

Veronica: And now he's lost in this storm.

Sabina: He knows his way around those woods.

Veronica: What if he doesn't want to be found?

Sabina: Veronica, did you have sex with Cole?

Veronica: No I did not.

Sabina: Don't lie to me girl.

Veronica: I didn't!

Cole enters.

Cole: Not a sign. Leslie's looking now.

Veronica: Did you see Forest?

Cole: I thought so, but I wasn't sure.

Sabina: Are you proud of yourself young man?

Cole: I never wanted this to happen.

Sabina: If that were true it wouldn't have. Aren't you people old enough to recognize hormones? Why did you come back?

Cole: I love your daughter, Miss Sabina.

Sabina: Shut up!

There is a crash of thunder. Forest enters.

Sabina: Well at least you have the good sense to come in out of the rain.

Veronica: Did you see him?

Forest: No.

Veronica: Nothing?

Forest: Nothing.

Pause.

Cole: Maybe Leslie will have better luck.

Forest: Maybe.

Sabina: You must both get out of those wet things immediately.

Forest: I'm fine.

Sabina: Lottie, take Cole to Sam's suite.

Lottie: Yes'm. Come on, Mr. Cole. We'll get you some dry things.

Cole and Lottie exit.

Forest: I'll go back to the garage. Let me know if you hear anything.

Sabina: Of course.

Forest exits.

Sabina: Veronica, stop worrying.

Veronica: I can't, Momma. I have a bad feeling about this.

SCENE 17

The garage. Darkness. The door opens and someone enters, stands for a moment, breathing heavily.

Acker: Are you here?

Forest: Let me get the light.

Forest turns on a dim light.

Acker: I feel like someone's reached down my throat and tried to pull my insides out.

Forest: Leslie's very worried.

Acker: He'll get tired and come in soon enough.

Forest: Yes.

Acker: I'm not giving up without a fight, Forest. Not this time. If Cole thinks he can waltz off with Veronica and have me be a perfect gentleman, he's dead wrong.

Forest: It won't be easy.

Acker: I know. And I'll probably fail, but I've still got to try. I'll show her. I love her, Forest. I do. Even now. After what I saw. I want Veronica to know – to see – that I tried. At least I cared enough to try.

Forest: She has no soul.

Acker: What?

Forest: She's empty inside. Barren.

Acker: She isn't.

Forest: She doesn't love you. She doesn't love Cole. She doesn't love anyone.

Acker: How can you say that?

Forest: She asked me to kill you.

Long pause.

Acker: You're lying.

Pause.

Acker: No you're not.

Pause.

Acker: She would take that chance for Cole?

Forest: I don't think Cole has anything to do with it.

Acker: Are you going to?

Pause.

Forest: I'll make it quick.

Acker: I'll fight.

Forest: It's pointless, Acker.

Forest extends his hand to Acker.

Forest: Come with me.

Acker: No. Please.

Acker takes Forest's outstretched hand.

Acker: I can't.

Forest: It'll be peaceful.

Acker: No.

Forest: You'll go somewhere nice.

Acker: Please.

Forest: Where everyone is beautiful.

Acker: You'll both pay!!

Forest takes Acker's head in his hands and turns it sharply. Acker's neck breaks with a sickening crack. Forest drags Acker off into the darkness. Forest is heard breathing heavily. The sound of the storm has receded, there is a knock at the door and Leslie enters. He glances around.

Leslie: Forest?

Forest enters drying his hands on a towel.

Forest: Right here.

Leslie: I thought he might've come back.

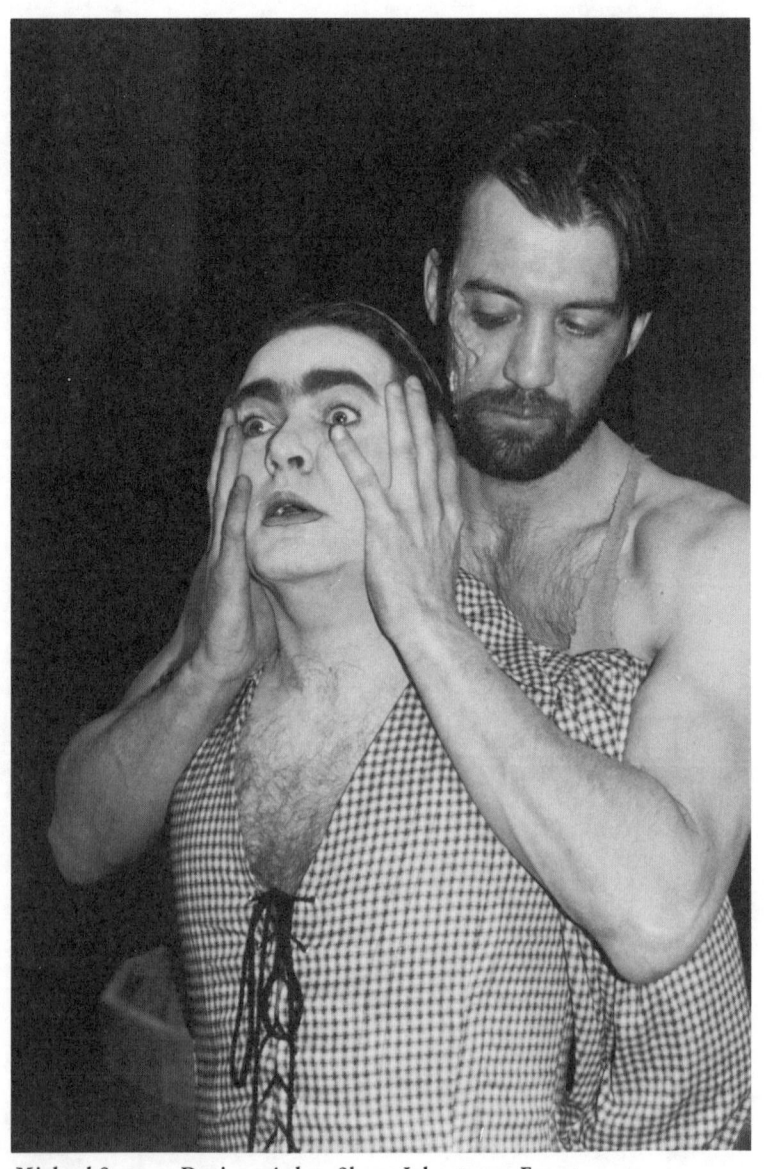

Michael Spencer-Davis as Acker, Shaun Johnston as Forest.

Forest: Everything'll work out, Les.

Leslie: Goddamn Cole can't keep his hands off anyone.

Forest moves behind Leslie and massages his shoulders.

Forest: Just relax.

Leslie: I'll try.

Forest moves closer and whispers in Leslie's ear from behind.

Forest: Your shirt is soaked.

Leslie: I know.

Forest: Let's take it off.

Forest removes Leslie's shirt, allowing his hands to linger over Leslie's body.

Leslie: This place is full of horrible people.

Forest: Most places are.

Leslie: Acker needed her.

Forest: What do you need, Les?

Leslie: Contact.

Leslie reaches out and touches Forest's chest. Forest moves Leslie's hand to his crotch. Leslie massages it, staring into Forest's face.

Forest: I hope you like it rough.

Leslie: Sure.

Forest: Not in the light.

Leslie: I don't mind looking at you.

Forest: That's not the problem.

Forest leads Leslie off into the darkness.

Leslie: What's that smell?

Forest: Nothing.

SCENE 18

The drawing-room. Cole is changed and sipping a hot toddy. Veronica enters and goes to the window. They do not look at one another.

Cole: I wish we'd had time to tell him.

Veronica: We didn't.

Pause.

Veronica: It's hit Mother the hardest.

Cole: You couldn't have gone ahead with the wedding, Veronica.

Pause.

Veronica: Do you want to marry me now?

Cole: If you don't mind what people will say.

Veronica: I don't care about people, Cole.

SCENE 19

The garage. Night. Forest and Leslie enter from the darkness, adjusting their clothing.

Leslie: Am I bleeding?

Forest: Just a bit.

Leslie: Can I spend the night?

Forest: I don't... like to sleep with other people.

Leslie: It's not me?

Forest: Good night, Les.

Leslie: Good night, Forest.

Leslie exits. Forest locks the door after him. He then takes a saw and an axe from the workbench and exits into the darkness. Sound of something wet being cut by a saw. After a moment there is a knock at the door. Forest enters carrying the saw, his hands covered with blood. Veronica enters.

Veronica: Did he turn up? Did you... *She notices the blood on his hands.* Oh, thank God.

Forest: I'll make sure the body's never found.

Veronica: You'll have to do something about the smell.

Forest: Don't worry.

Veronica: Did he – fight?

Forest: Yes.

Veronica: Did he scream?

Forest: Yes.

Veronica: It must have been horrible.

Forest: Must've been.

Pause.

Veronica: Cole asked me to marry him.

Forest: Congratulations.

Pause.

Veronica: This was the only way, wasn't it?

Forest: You seemed to think so.

Veronica: Everyone will assume he ran away... or something.

Pause.

Veronica: Of course I'll pay you.

Pause.

Veronica: Name your price.

She nervously glances at Forest's bloody hands.

Veronica: How much?

Forest flexes his hands.

Veronica: You really should clean up.

Forest raises his hands toward Veronica.

Veronica: How – how much do you want?

Forest sets his hands on Veronica's breasts. She stares at them.

Veronica: We're – we're – we're very rich.

Forest grabs her and pulls her close.

Veronica: Please. Don't.

Forest grabs Veronica by the hair and pulls her face very close to his.

Forest: Kiss me.

Veronica: I can't.

Forest: Do it.

Veronica: You're an ugly man.

Forest: Kiss me.

Veronica: Please. Anything else.

Forest: Everything else.

Veronica sinks to her knees with her hands on Forest's belt.

Forest: I can smell you.

Veronica: Please.

Forest: Your skin. Your breasts. Your stomach.

As Forest speaks Veronica takes each of his fingers in her mouth and sucks the blood off them.

Forest: Your neck. Your back. Your thighs. The heat of you. I smell your juices. The taste of your skin. Your blood.

Veronica has finished sucking his fingers.

Veronica: Forest, I'm a virgin.

Forest: I don't mind.

Veronica: No! It's mine! I'm saving it.

Forest: I just killed someone for you.

Veronica: I'll scream.

Forest: Go ahead.

Pause.

Forest: You're mine, Veronica.

Veronica: No. Please.

Forest extends his hand to Veronica. She stares at him.

Forest: Body and soul.

Veronica: Please. I can't.

Forest takes Veronica's hand, smearing it with blood. Veronica stares at his hand for a long moment.

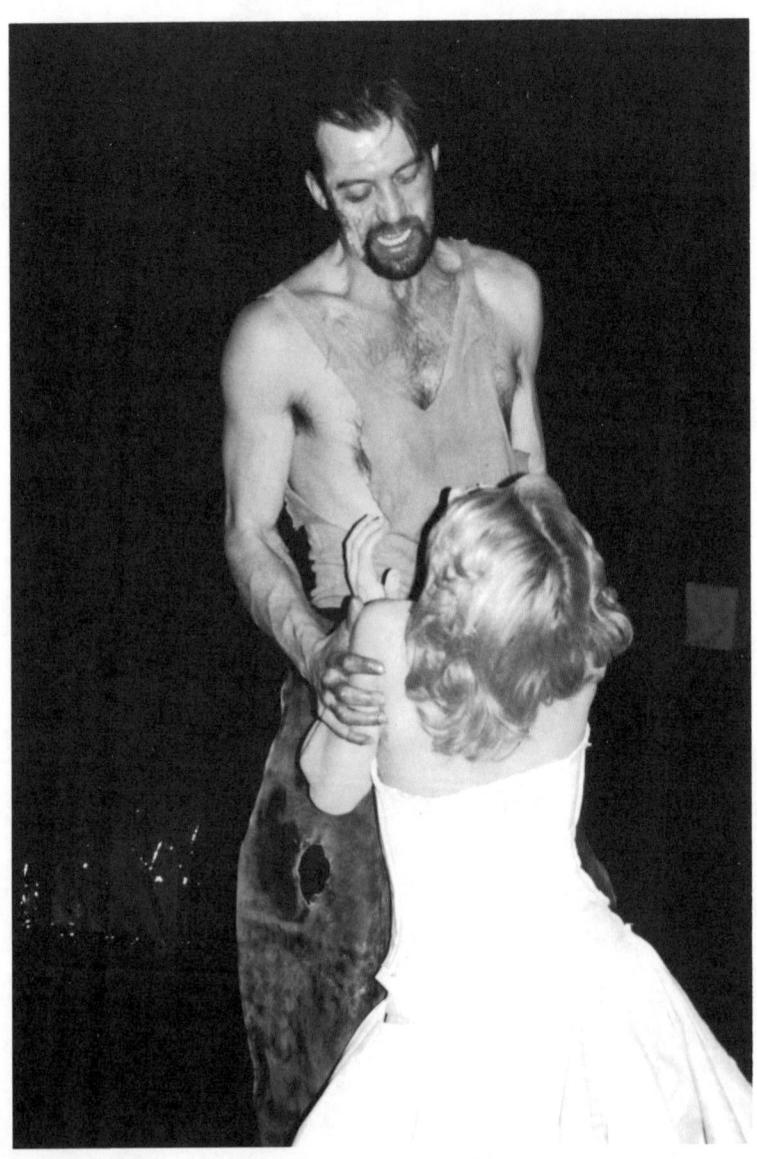

Kate Ryan as Veronica, Shaun Johnston as Forest.

Veronica: Yes.

Forest: Yes.

Forest leads Veronica off into the darkness. They are both breathing very heavily. The storm crashes outside.

SCENE 20

The drawing-room. Morning. Lottie is watering the plants. Leslie enters.

Lottie: Mr. Cole? Oh. Mr. Leslie.

Leslie: Has anyone found my brother yet?

Lottie: 'fraid not.

Leslie: Where's Cole?

Lottie: The guest room.

Leslie: You sure?

Lottie: Put him there myself.

Sabina enters.

Sabina: You needn't worry, Leslie. I'll do my best to insure there's no more hanky panky on this ranch.

Leslie: I'm gonna call the cops.

Sabina: Too late. They're out there right now. How are your parents taking it?

Leslie: They're old, Miss Sabina. Not well.

Sabina: I'll send a note over with one of the boys. I know it won't change anything, but it's the least I can do.

Leslie: I guess Cole'll be staying here now.

Sabina: Why don't we have Lottie wake him up so we can ask him ourselves?

Lottie: *Exiting.* Yes'm.

Leslie: Goddamn Cole.

Sabina: Don't. Things are bad enough already.

Leslie: What if Acker doesn't come back.

Sabina: He will.

Forest enters.

Sabina: Have those cops managed to do anything besides trample my rosebushes into the mud?

Forest: No. They're finished in the woods and want to start on the outbuildings.

Sabina: Good. Keep an eye on them. Now if you'll excuse me gentlemen, I think it's time I woke my daughter.

Sabina exits.

Leslie: What are you smiling about?

Forest: Last night.

Leslie: Me too.

Forest: Oh. Right.

Cole enters.

Cole: Still no Acker.

Leslie: At least the rain's slowed down.

Forest: And washed away any trail he might have left.

Leslie: I didn't think of that.

Forest: I'd better get back out there.

Leslie: I'll come.

Forest: Best to let me and the cops take care of this, Les.

Leslie: Okay.

Forest exits.

Leslie: I suppose you're gonna tell me you love her.

Cole: I find her irresistible.

Leslie: And her lifestyle?

Cole: Don't be bitter.

Leslie: Cole, am I supposed to forget everything we've ever done?

Cole: If that's what it takes.

Leslie: You're going to marry her.

Cole: Yes.

Leslie: Just couldn't resist the set up, could you?

Cole: I love her.

Leslie: You don't know what it means.

Cole: At least I don't mistake boys' games for the real thing.

Leslie: Be careful.

Cole: Why aren't you out mooning over the gargoyle in the garage.

Leslie: He's twice the man you'll ever be.

Cole: I hated it when you touched me, Leslie. I only did it because I felt sorry for you.

Leslie: Shut up!

Veronica enters.

Veronica: What's all the noise about?

Leslie: Cole, if anything's happened to my brother you're going to pay!

Leslie exits. Sabina enters.

Sabina: This is not what I want to be hearing this morning.

Veronica: It's Leslie.

Sabina: The boy's bound to be upset.

Veronica: It's not like it's our fault.

Veronica moves to Cole and nudges him.

Cole: Miss Sabina, we have something to tell you.

Sabina: No you don't.

Cole: I want to marry your daughter.

Sabina: I will not listen to this.

Veronica: He loves me.

Sabina: So did Acker.

Veronica: I'm marrying him, Momma.

Sabina: Excuse me.

Veronica: Don't you dare leave this room! I want to get married.

Sabina: Not now, Veronica.

Veronica: Yes now! Right now. I'm going to marry Cole.

Sabina stops, but doesn't look at Veronica.

Veronica: Momma?

Sabina: Haven't I always given you everything you want?

Veronica embraces Sabina.

Veronica: Oh – thank you, Momma.

Sabina: Excuse me.

Sabina exits.

Veronica: What a grouch.

Cole moves to Veronica and puts his arms around her.

Cole: She's upset about Acker.

Veronica: Oh Cole, we're going to get married.

Cole: I can't wait. A virgin.

Veronica laughs nervously.

SCENE 21

Sabina's office. Afternoon. Standing on the desk is a dressmaker's dummy with a wedding dress. Lottie is repairing a seam.

Sabina: Lottie, that's antique lace!

Lottie: Sorry, Ma'am.

Sabina: Are you trembling?

Lottie: A bit.

Sabina: I'm sorry for shouting at you, Lottie. Seeing that dress again has upset me.

Lottie: It's beautiful.

Sabina: I hope it brings her more happiness than it brought me. If only Acker had been man enough to come back for her.

There is a knock at the door.

Jill Dyck as Sabina, Kate Newby as Lottie.

Sabina: Enter.

Forest enters.

Forest: Everything you ordered is in the kitchen.

Sabina: Thank you.

Forest stares at the dress for a long moment.

Sabina: Forest?

Forest: Yes?

Sabina: Are you all right?

Forest: Yes. Excuse me.

Forest exits.

Lottie: This rain makes everybody crazy.

SCENE 22

The veranda. Night. Cole and Veronica are there.

Veronica: Over half the guests have cancelled.

Cole: Well, you are missing Acker's clan.

Veronica: I wanted a big wedding.

Cole takes her in his arms.

Cole: I'll be there.

Veronica: Yes.

Cole notices something on Veronica's shoulder and examines it.

Cole: What's this?

Veronica: Nothing.

Cole: It looks like a bruise.

Veronica: I – I bumped into something.

Cole: Darling, you've got to be more careful.

Lottie enters. She sees them and stops and stares.

Veronica: Lottie?

Cole: What is it?

Lottie: I'm sorry.

Lottie exits.

Veronica: What's with her?

Cole: Who knows?

Veronica: Kiss me.

Cole kisses her.

Veronica: Harder.

Cole kisses her again.

SCENE 23

The garage. Night. It is dark. There is a muffled sound, like someone laughing or crying. Forest is heard off.

Forest: Hello?

Forest enters, turning the light on.

Forest: Who's there?

The sound fades. There is a knock at the door. Forest opens it. Veronica enters.

Veronica: Why's the door locked?

Forest: I wasn't expecting you tonight.

Veronica: What did you do with the body?

Forest: I fed his flesh to the hogs and burnt the bones.

Veronica: Excellent.

Forest: Just a minute.

Veronica: What?

Forest exits into the darkness. He returns with something held behind his back.

Forest: I saved this for you.

Veronica: You didn't.

Forest produces a skull from behind his back.

Veronica: You did!

Forest: I wanted you to see what your handsome Acker looked like on the inside.

Veronica: Let me hold it.

Forest tosses her the skull. She examines it.

Veronica: You've got to stop leaving marks. Cole noticed.

Forest: I'll be more careful.

Veronica: I want it to stop.

Forest: You only ever complain afterwards.

Veronica: I mean it...

Forest: *Cutting her off.* Why did you come out here to tell me all of this now, Veronica? You could've caught me anywhere.

Veronica: I have to go.

Forest: No.

Forest reaches out and touches Veronica's nipples. She stops speaking abruptly.

Forest: Take your clothes off, Veronica.

Pause. Veronica slowly begins to undo her blouse.

SCENE 24

The drawing-room. Sabina is working on a needlepoint. Lottie is looking out the window.

Sabina: Lottie, are Veronica and Cole staying in their respective rooms at night?

Lottie: Yes'm. I make sure myself.

Sabina: I thought I heard someone moving around last night.

Lottie: Old houses make noises, Miss Sabina. I remember...

Lottie stops speaking suddenly and peers out the window.

Sabina: What is it?

Sabina moves to the window.

Lottie: Thought I saw something. Over by the trees.

Sabina: I can't see anything.

Lottie: It was just quick. I don't know.

Sabina: Do you think Acker might be out there? Hiding? Watching us?

Lottie: Doesn't sound much like Mr. Acker.

Sabina: Make sure all the doors are bolted tonight.

Pause.

Sabina: Lottie, I'm going to use that potion on Veronica.

Lottie: You think she's done it?

Sabina: It might explain why everything's gotten so strange. Lottie, I'd swear you were looking for someone out there.

Lottie: Just looking.

SCENE 25

The garage. Night. Veronica sits in a chair. Forest stands behind her, touching her lightly.

Veronica: I don't want to do this.

Forest: Why's your heart beating so fast then?

Veronica: You're a horrible, ugly, hateful man.

Forest: I'm also as hard as a rock and out of my mind with the smell of you.

Pause.

Veronica: *Quietly.* You shouldn't talk to me like that.

Forest: You have goose bumps. Are you excited?

Veronica: You ugly bastard.

Forest: Kiss me.

Veronica: I'd sooner die.

Forest: Veronica, you've done things with me that would embarrass a whore. But you still won't kiss me.

Veronica: It's the only thing you can't take from me.

Forest: It's that important?

Veronica: As long as I don't kiss you and mean it, I'm still a virgin.

Pause.

Forest: You're changing the rules.

Veronica: That was always a rule. I just never told you.

Pause.

Forest: If you kiss me I'll go away. Leave you alone. Forever.

Pause.

Veronica: Why aren't you like other men?

Forest: Do I look like other men?

Forest moves to Veronica and begins to fondle her. He produces a length of rope from his pocket and binds Veronica's wrists with it.

Veronica: You're sick.

Forest: Yes.

Veronica: I hate you.

Forest: You smell like an animal right now.

Veronica: Yeah?

Forest: I'm going to put you down, Veronica. I'm going to put you down and sniff your private parts like a dog. I'm going to tangle one hand in your hair and stick my fingers in your mouth. I'm going to take you from behind. Hard. Deep. Just the way you like it.

Veronica has moved into a "doggy" position. Forest positions himself behind her and growls.

Veronica: *Moans.* Hard.

SCENE 26

The drawing-room. Night. Cole enters wearing his robe. He tiptoes into the room and listens for a moment.

Cole: Hello?

Lottie steps out of the shadows, wearing her nightclothes.

Lottie: Mr. Cole?

Cole: *Startled.* Lottie?!

Lottie: Everything okay?

Cole: Just a nightmare.

Cole's robe has fallen open slightly. Lottie stares at his body.

Lottie: My mama taught me a back rub that makes a body sleep like a baby.

Lottie moves toward Cole with her hands outstretched. Cole nearly lets her touch him, then pulls away at the last minute.

Cole: I'm okay. Thanks.

Lottie: Good night, Mr. Cole.

Lottie slips back into the shadows.

Cole: Good night.

SCENE 27

The garage. Night. Veronica is pulling her robe on. Forest is partially dressed.

Veronica: I hope you don't think this is going to continue after I'm married.

Forest: Cole thinks he's getting a virgin.

Veronica: You're jealous of him, aren't you.

Forest: He's a gigolo and a liar.

Veronica: He's very handsome.

Forest: He'll never be able to give you what you need.

Veronica: I have to go.

Forest: Veronica?...

Veronica: What?

Forest: Forget it.

Veronica: No. What were you going to say?

Forest: It really didn't matter to me if you were a virgin.

Pause.

Veronica: Why did you come here?

Forest: I wanted to get away.

Veronica: And then you wanted me.

Forest: I always get what I want.

Veronica: No one gets everything they want.

Forest: I do.

Veronica: Why?

Forest: Because I don't want much.

Pause.

Forest: We're a lot alike.

Veronica: I have to go.

Forest: I know.

SCENE 28

Sabina's office. Day. There is a knock at the door.

Sabina: Enter.

Leslie enters.

Leslie: Where's Forest?

Sabina: He took Veronica and Cole to the hair dresser. Why?

Leslie: I have to talk to him.

Sabina: What's on your mind?

Leslie: Do you believe in ghosts, Miss Sabina.

Sabina: Why do you ask?

Leslie: I keep having this dream. About Acker. He's standing by the edge of the woods. It's dark and windy. He keeps yelling something and pointing to the trees, only I can never quite hear what it is he's saying.

Sabina: The cops searched every inch of this ranch and those woods.

Leslie: We all know places around here where no one could find us, if that's what we wanted.

Sabina: Acker has run off somewhere to lick his wounds. Even the cops think so. People do it all the time.

Leslie: I think he's dead.

Pause.

Sabina: Come Leslie, we are both in need of a good, stiff drink.

Sabina leads Leslie off.

Sabina: We're having a bit of a celebration tomorrow.

Leslie: I don't have much to celebrate.

Sabina: Neither do I. Why don't you come? We'll be
depressed together.

They exit.

SCENE 29

*Veronica's room. Evening. Lottie is lacing Veronica into a
corset. Veronica wears pieces of her wedding ensemble.*

Veronica: *Pushing Lottie away.* Not so tight, stupid!

Lottie: Miss Veronica – really!

Veronica: I could hardly breathe.

Lottie: Sure is hard to tell it's the day before your wedding.

Veronica: *Struggling with her ties.* Damn it to hell – shit!

Sabina enters.

Sabina: What a charming choice of words.

Lottie: Careful. She's a regular monster tonight.

Veronica: I'm nervous.

Sabina: This wedding was your idea.

Veronica: Thanks for the sympathy.

Sabina: I don't approve. You can't expect me to.

Veronica: But it's just as if I was marrying Acker, only it's
Cole.

Sabina: Cole is a pretty face from nowhere. Do you really
think you can accept that?

Veronica: Yes! *Short pause.* You wouldn't disown me, would you, Momma?

Sabina: Probably not. Now if you'll excuse me I'm going to supervise the stuffing of artichoke hearts into mushroom caps. Come, Lottie.

Veronica: I still need her.

Sabina: Very well.

Sabina exits.

Veronica: She's in a mood.

Lottie: She's putting up with a lot with this wedding, Missy. If it doesn't all work out she's gonna be real unhappy.

Pause.

Veronica: Lottie?

Lottie: Yes'm?

Veronica: I'm sorry I was beastly to you earlier.

Lottie: I'm used to it.

Veronica: Can I tell you something I've never, ever told anyone else?

Lottie: I guess so.

Veronica: I'm not a virgin.

Lottie: What?!

Veronica: Remember when Momma put me in those riding lessons?

Lottie: That was years ago – Lordy! You mean...

Veronica: I didn't even realize it'd happened, until I saw the blood.

Lottie: Why didn't you tell someone?

Veronica: I was a kid. I was terrified. You know what Momma can be like.

Lottie: What's Mr. Cole gonna think?!

Veronica: Oh Lottie, I'm so scared. Momma will die. Cole will leave me!

Lottie: Don't cry, honey.

Veronica: I thought you might – might know of a potion or a poultice or something that would fix it.

Lottie: I don't know nothing like that.

Veronica: Oh no!

Lottie: I know another potion.

Veronica: What kind?

Lottie: Made from the stems of mushrooms and coleus leaves. It clouds the head. Makes things fuzzy.

Veronica: You mean he might not notice?

Lottie: Not that fuzzy. But fuzzy enough so if someone stepped in for you – someone who was a virgin – he might not know the difference.

Veronica: But I don't know any virgins!

Pause.

Lottie: You know me, Miss Veronica.

Pause.

Veronica: Oh Lottie, I couldn't possibly let you do something like that for me.

Lottie: I just want you and Mr. Cole to be happy together.

Pause.

Veronica: We'd have to be very careful.

Lottie: Yes.

Veronica: *Suddenly embracing Lottie.* Darling. Thank you. But I must give you some money. To make up for what you're losing. Just let me find my cheque book.

Lottie: Oh no. I couldn't.

Veronica: *Writing cheque.* Is five thousand enough?

Lottie: That's plenty.

Veronica: Here.

Veronica hands Lottie a cheque.

Lottie: Oh no!

Veronica: What?

Lottie: Your momma, I made her a potion too. To tell whether a lady is a virgin or not!

Veronica: *Snatching cheque back.* You did what?!

Lottie: She asked me to give it to you in your champagne. After dinner.

Veronica: That conniving bitch. What does this potion do if you're a virgin?

Lottie: Nothing.

Veronica: And if you're not?

Lottie: Makes you crazy. Big crazy.

Veronica: Can you switch the potion?

Lottie: Your mama's got it with her. She'd know.

Veronica: But if I drink this stuff and lose my mind I'll give it away for sure!

Lottie: I'll drink it.

Veronica: You?

Lottie: I'll switch the glasses after she's poured it. It won't do nothing to me.

Veronica: Lottie, you're so clever. Serve the old cow right too. Oh Lottie – thank you. Thank you. You're my best friend.

Veronica gives the cheque back to Lottie.

Lottie: You're my best friend too, Miss Veronica.

Veronica: Now hang all this stuff up. I'm going to knock their eyes out tomorrow.

Veronica exits. Lottie holds the wedding dress up in front of her body and smiles, humming softly.

SCENE 30

The garage. Night. Forest is working on engine parts. There is a muffled noise, like someone quietly laughing or crying, from outside the light. Forest straightens up and listens.

Forest: Who is it?

A quiet murmur from the darkness.

Forest: Say something.

A figure is seen dimly, moving just out of the perimeter of the light.

Forest: Veronica?

The figure retreats. Acker's skull suddenly rolls into the light, stopping at Forest's feet.

Forest: Ah.

Forest picks up the skull.

Forest: It is you.

Acker: *Off. Ghostly.* Revenge.

Forest: Revenge?

Forest sticks his fingers through the skull's eyes and rolls it back into the darkness, as if it were a bowling ball.

Forest: I doubt it.

SCENE 31

The drawing-room. Night. Sabina and Lottie are there. There is a bottle of champagne and glasses on a tray. Sabina holds the vial of potion.

Sabina: *Pouring potion into glass.* Now please remember. It's this one.

Lottie: Yes'm.

Sabina: There are no ill effects are there?

Lottie: She won't even remember.

Sabina: Excellent.

Lottie: Miss Sabina?

Sabina: Yes?

Lottie: Would you mind if I had a glass too?

Sabina: I guess not. After all, you're nearly one of the family. Now, take this out of here and put it in the icebox so it doesn't go flat. And remember, it's that glass.

Lottie: *Exiting.* Yes'm.

Cole and Veronica enter.

Sabina: You are a lovely couple.

Veronica: Does that mean you're not mad at us anymore?

Sabina: Tell me Cole, were you planning to take Veronica back east with you and set up a new life there?

Cole: I haven't considered it yet.

Sabina: I couldn't bear it. I'm far too old and rich and lonely to live here by myself. If you promise me the two of you will stay here, I'll make sure you're very well cared for.

Veronica: What?

Sabina: Who knows Cole, perhaps I'll even teach you a few things. Show you the ropes. You know.

Veronica: Cole isn't interested.

Sabina: No?

Cole: We should hear your mother out.

Sabina: Tell me Cole, how thrilled were your parents to hear about this sudden wedding?

Cole: Not very.

Sabina: And what exactly have you been taking in school?

Cole: Uh – general arts.

Sabina: How practical.

Veronica: Momma – stop.

Sabina: Darling, surely you're not trying to convince me that you might actually "make a go of it" in some cockroach ridden flat in the east?

Veronica: Well – no.

Sabina: Then let Cole speak for himself.

Veronica: You don't have any money?

Cole: Well – no.

Sabina: Then it's settled. I will support the two of you and you will bless me with your constant companionship.

Cole: Yes.

Sabina: Fabulous. Self-sufficiency can be so tedious.

Veronica: Cole?

Leslie enters.

Sabina: Leslie – so glad you could make it.

Cole: Did you come to wish us luck?

Leslie: I came because Miss Sabina asked me to.

Sabina: Leslie is a gracious man.

Lottie enters with champagne glasses on a tray.

Sabina: Impeccable timing. A toast. Chandon Brut. 1936. Very nice.

As Lottie distributes the glasses she and Veronica share a confidential look. Lottie gives Sabina a glass and winks at her. Sabina raises her glass.

Sabina: Now...

Forest enters.

Forest: Oh. Sorry.

Sabina: Lottie, get Forest a glass, this instant.

Lottie: *Exiting.* Yes'm.

Sabina: We are celebrating.

Forest: Oh?

Sabina: Making the best of an unfortunate situation.

Veronica: Mother, are you okay?

Sabina: Absolutely.

Lottie enters with a glass of champagne.

Lottie: There you are, Mr. Forest.

Forest: Thank you, Lottie.

Sabina: *Raising her glass.* Now...

Sabina stops suddenly, noticing something in her glass.

Sabina: *To Lottie.* Are you trying to make me sick.

Lottie: What?

Sabina: There is a hair floating in my champagne.

Lottie: Miss Sabina – I'm sorry!

Sabina: Give me your glass.

Sabina goes to take Lottie's glass. Veronica steps in, handing Sabina her glass.

Veronica: No – take mine.

Sabina: Nonsense. This toast has already gone on too long.

Sabina hands Veronica her glass and takes Lottie's glass.

Leslie: It's only a hair. I'll take it out.

Leslie takes Sabina's glass and hands his to Lottie. Sabina grabs a glass from Lottie.

Sabina: Give me that! Now.

Veronica and Lottie look at one another in horror. Who has the potion?

Cole: To Veronica. And her mother.

Sabina: To our future.

All raise their glasses. All drink. Pause. Veronica and Lottie watch Sabina carefully.

Cole: Marvelous bead.

Leslie: I'm sorry, Miss Sabina. I really can't –

Sabina rubs her head, looking suddenly faint.

Veronica: Momma?...

Sabina: Just a twinge.

Forest: *Leading Sabina to a chair.* Sabina, you'd better...

Sabina suddenly pushes Forest away with a wild laugh.

Sabina: Lying pricks!

Lottie: Miss Sabina!

Leslie: Someone call a doctor.

Veronica: No. It'll pass.

Sabina: Telling you they love you. Telling you anything to make you part with your treasures. Feeding you sweet words and tired lines. Breathing in your ear and nuzzling your neck. Trying to get into your wet areas and stick pointy things in and you're supposed to pretend it doesn't hurt when it does and then you bleed and just when it starts to feel good they're finished but they think you belong to them now and they can stick it in whenever they want to and all you can think about are the rumours and that story of the woman with her babies and how they burned!

Pause. Sabina calms suddenly. The others are all staring at her.

Sabina: Did I smear my lipstick?

Cole: No.

Sabina: Everything all right?

Veronica: Oh yes, Momma, everything's fine.

Leslie: What?

Veronica: Just a dizzy spell.

Leslie: I can't stay here. I'll talk to you later, Forest. Thanks for the champagne.

Leslie exits quickly.

Sabina: Oh dear – he's more upset than I thought.

Cole: Leslie's a sensitive man.

Sabina: Ronnie, did you enjoy the champagne, Darling?

Veronica: It was delicious.

Sabina suddenly goes to Veronica and embraces her.

Sabina: You're the best daughter a mother could hope for. I don't know why I ever doubted you.

Veronica: Doubted me?

Sabina: I'm a malicious old woman. You and Cole are free to live wherever you want to. I'll help in any way I can.

Cole: We'd like to live here.

Sabina: Take some time. Think about it.

Cole: We'd like to live here.

Forest: Excuse me.

Sabina: Of course. We have a big day ahead of us tomorrow.

Forest: Good night. *Looking directly at Veronica.* Good night, Veronica.

Veronica: Goodbye, Forest.

Brief pause. Forest exits.

Lottie: Mr. Forest's not going anywhere?

Veronica: What?

Lottie: You said goodbye.

Veronica: Did I? *Brittle laugh.* My mistake.

Sabina: Darling, why don't you and Lottie turn in now. I'd like a word with my future son-in-law.

Veronica: Of course.

Sabina: Good night, Baby.

Veronica: 'night, Sweetie.

Lottie: 'night.

Veronica and Lottie begin to exit.

Cole: Veronica?

Veronica: Yes?

Cole: Good night.

Veronica: Oh. Good night.

Lottie: 'night, Mr. Cole.

Lottie and Veronica exit.

Sabina: I don't trust you, Cole. You're too pretty for a man, and you have a weak hairline.

Cole: I have no control over my head.

Sabina: I had someone check you out. Your parents don't know a thing about this wedding. In fact, your parents haven't heard from you in three years. You don't attend school either. Who's been supporting you? Leslie perhaps?

Cole: I love your daughter, Miss Sabina.

Sabina: Good. Because, if you hurt her, you'll be very sorry.

Cole: I could never hurt her.

Sabina: You've been dreaming about Acker too, haven't you?

Cole: How did you know that?

Sabina: Leslie's convinced he's dead.

Pause.

Sabina: Do you think he's dead?

Pause.

Cole: He could be.

Pause.

Sabina: Go to bed, Cole.

Cole: Good night.

Cole exits. Sabina pours herself a drink and moves to the window, gazing out of it thoughtfully.

SCENE 32

Veronica's bedroom. Night. Lottie is brushing Veronica's hair.

Veronica: Lottie, I think it's a little strange that this potion will confuse Cole enough not to know who he's with, but not enough for him to tell if she's a virgin.

Lottie: Potions are potions, Missy.

Veronica: I almost died when Momma took that glass.

Lottie: Lucky she doesn't remember.

Veronica: Yes. Now look, tomorrow night I'll wear my sheer night-gown with the marabou trim.

Lottie: And I'll wear the other one, just like it.

Veronica: I'll slip out to make myself more comfortable.

Lottie: And I'll slip in.

Veronica: Exactly.

Lottie: What about your momma?

Veronica: Leave her to me. I'll make sure she gets a good night's sleep.

Lottie: You been slipping her pills?

Veronica: Mind your business.

Cole knocks then enters quickly.

Cole: Darling.

Veronica: That will be all, Lottie.

Lottie stops brushing Veronica's hair.

Lottie: Yes'm.

Pause.

Veronica: You may go.

Lottie: Yes'm. 'night, Mr. Cole.

Cole: Good night.

Lottie exits.

Cole: You're mad at me.

Veronica: Not at all.

Cole: I've never had anything, Veronica. Never.

Veronica: I understand.

Cole: You don't know what it's like to want things. Things you've never had.

Veronica: No, but it's all right.

He kisses her.

Cole: I would never – ever – do anything to hurt you.

Cole gets on his knees before Veronica and takes her hand. Short pause.

Veronica: Of course you wouldn't.

Cole cuddles up to her.

Cole: We could get an early start on tomorrow night.

Veronica pulls away from Cole sadly.

Veronica: I doubt it.

SCENE 33

The garage. Night. Forest sits in the light, drinking a beer. Acker's ghost is heard, off.

Acker: Revenge.

Forest: Go to sleep, Acker.

Acker: *Fading.* Revenge.

There is a knock at the door. Forest smiles and goes to it quickly.

Forest: I knew you wouldn't be able to stay away.

Forest opens the door. His smile fades. Leslie enters.

Leslie: I have to talk to you.

Forest: Not now.

Leslie: Forest, I think someone murdered my brother!

Forest allows Leslie to enter and closes the door.

Forest: Why do you think that?

Leslie: I've been having these dreams.

Forest: That's not too concrete, pal.

Leslie: He's always at the edge of the woods, trying to tell me something.

Forest: Who would want to kill Acker?

Leslie: Cole and Veronica.

Forest: Why wouldn't they just run off?

Leslie: Miss Sabina's money. Cole likes money.

Forest: Okay – look – don't say anything about this. Let me keep my eyes on things. If it's true he's bound to slip up somewhere.

Leslie: Thanks.

Pause.

Leslie: I thought you were mad at me or something.

Forest: *Moving behind Leslie.* Never.

Leslie: I think about you all the time.

Forest: *Stroking Leslie's body.* I think about you too.

Leslie: There's something weird happening here. The way Miss Sabina acted –

Forest puts his hand over Leslie's mouth. His other hand is beneath Leslie's shirt.

Forest: Sssh. Just keep your mouth shut. We'll never catch Cole if he thinks we suspect anything. Okay?

Leslie nods. Forest removes his hand from Leslie's mouth and leads Leslie off into the darkness.

Forest: Come on. I've got some fresh motor oil.

Forest and Leslie exit. Acker's ghost appears on the edge of the light.

Acker: Revenge.

SCENE 34

The veranda. Morning. Sabina enters from the house, dressed for a wedding. She looks at the sky and smiles. Veronica enters, dressed for marriage.

Sabina: Baby, you've never looked lovelier.

Veronica: You're sure? My make-up's fabulous? This nail colour's not too bright?

Sabina: You're breathtaking.

Veronica: Don't cry. You'll make everyone sad and ruin everything.

Sabina: I'm sorry.

Forest enters in his dress uniform.

Forest: The car is waiting.

Sabina: Damn! I forgot Grandpa Martin's boutonnière in the pantry.

Sabina exits.

Forest: What's he going to think? Tonight?

Veronica: It's taken care of.

Forest: You'll never be yourself.

Veronica: I don't care.

Forest: Don't marry him, Veronica.

Veronica: I have to now.

Forest: He's using you.

Veronica: And what are you doing to me, Forest?

Forest: I said you were mine and I meant it.

Forest grabs Veronica by the shoulders.

Veronica: Not anymore.

Forest: You like it as much as I do.

Veronica: No!

Forest: Leslie thinks Acker was murdered!

Veronica: Then kill him.

Sabina enters. Forest and Veronica do not see her.

Veronica: You don't own me.

Sabina: Take your hands off my daughter.

Forest lets go of Veronica. Pause.

Veronica: I tripped. He was – was helping me.

Long pause.

Veronica: Well – let's get married.

Forest and Veronica exit. Sabina stands watching them.

SCENE 35

Night. Veronica's room. It is now filled with flowers. Lottie is in the process of turning down the bed. She sprays a bit of perfume in the air. She smiles and hums a few bars from the Carpenters' "We've Only Just Begun." Sabina enters.

Sabina: You sound festive this evening.

Lottie: I do love weddings.

Sabina: Don't ever marry, Lottie. Don't have children.

Lottie: Miss Sabina, what a thing to say. Anyway, I've taken care of Miss Veronica for so long I almost feel like this is my wedding too.

Cole and Veronica enter noisily.

Veronica: Momma, you're not leaving already.

Sabina: I'm unusually tired tonight.

Veronica: It's been a radical day.

Sabina: Yes. Good night.

Cole: Good night – Mother.

Sabina exits.

Lottie: Good night, Mr. Cole.

Lottie exits. Cole closes the door after her and begins to pull his clothes off.

Cole: I've never seen your mother look so old.

Veronica: Did you see all the lovely presents I got?

Cole: You've got the only present I'm interested in.

Cole falls onto the bed, pulling Veronica with him.

Veronica: Oh look, Lottie left us something to drink.

Cole: I've had quite enough to drink.

Veronica: Darling, you don't understand. Lottie's got a way with herbs. She said this would... enhance things.

Cole: Let's have it then.

Veronica pours two glasses of potion from a beaker beside the bed. She gives Cole his glass.

Veronica: Drink it all.

Cole: Aren't you having any?

Veronica: Of course. But first I'm going to slip into something – more comfortable.

Cole drains his glass as Veronica exits. Veronica turns the lights down as she leaves.

Cole: What a babe. What a house. What a set up. Oh – hell – all fuzzy.

A light comes through the window. A distant voice is heard moaning "revenge." It is nearly inaudible. Cole moves to the window.

Cole: What's that? Nothing. Nothing out there but forest. Miles and miles of ugly old forest. *He laughs.* Ugly old Forest.

The light fades. Cole falls back onto the bed – grabs the other glass of potion and drinks it.

Cole: Well Acker, as usual, the best man won.

Lottie enters dressed as Veronica.

Cole: Babe, I'm outa my mind.

Lottie moves onto the bed. They kiss and nuzzle. Cole strokes her body.

Cole: Oh, Honey, you're ready.

Lottie: Uh huh.

Cole: I'll be gentle.

Lottie: Oh – that's okay.

SCENE 36

The garage. Night. Forest and Leslie are there.

Leslie: You're quiet tonight.

Forest: Yes.

Leslie: Do you like weddings?

Forest: No.

Leslie: Wouldn't you like to have someone? Someone to share your life with?

Pause.

Forest: No.

Leslie: I used to think maybe Cole would be that person for me.

Forest: You haven't got enough money, Les.

Leslie: It wasn't just the money.

Forest: Yes it was.

Pause.

Leslie: You never talk about your family.

Forest: Not my kind of people.

Leslie: Where are they?

Forest: Dead.

Leslie: All of them?

Forest: There was a fire.

Leslie: I'm sorry.

Forest: Don't be. *Short pause.* I didn't know them.

SCENE 37

The drawing-room. Night. Veronica paces quietly. She glances at her watch from time to time. Lottie enters, smiling and singing the Carpenters' "Close To You" softly to herself.

Veronica: Is he still awake?

Lottie: You bet.

Veronica: You could at least have the decency to stop smiling so much.

Lottie: Sorry.

Veronica: Everything that happened tonight.

Lottie: Yes?

Veronica: Forget it.

Lottie: I don't think I can.

Veronica: Try!

SCENE 38

The garage. Night. Leslie and Forest are there.

Leslie: Well I guess Cole's gotten what he wants by now.

Forest: Shut up!

Leslie: You want me to go?

Forest: No. I want to tie you up and bruise you in places only we'll know about.

Leslie: You make me do things I've never done before.

Forest: I don't make you do anything.

Leslie: I've never done them for anyone else.

Forest: Has anyone else asked?

Leslie: No.

Forest moves behind Leslie and pulls his hands behind his back.

Leslie: Where did you learn all this stuff?

Pause. Forest pulls a length of rope from his pocket.

Forest: Everywhere.

SCENE 39

The bedroom. Cole is in bed. Veronica enters and joins him.

Veronica: Was it – okay?

Cole: Magical.

Veronica: Oh. Good.

Cole: So gentle. It was the best experience of my life.

Veronica: Great.

Cole: Everything okay?

Veronica: Kiss me.

He kisses her.

Veronica: Harder.

He kisses her harder.

Veronica: Harder!

Veronica grabs Cole and kisses him rough and hard. Cole pulls away.

Cole: Hey!

Veronica: Let's do it again.

Cole: Wasn't four enough?

Veronica: Four?

Cole: I'm so tired.

Veronica: Cole.

Cole: *Falling asleep.* In the morning...

Veronica: But Cole...

Cole snores once, loudly. She shakes him. He is oblivious.

Veronica softly touches his face and looks at it closely. She pulls away from Cole.

Veronica: Forest.

SCENE 40

The garage. Night. Forest sits in a chair, toying with the rope. Leslie lies on the floor, partially dressed.

Leslie: That was incredible.

Forest suddenly moves behind Leslie and puts the rope around his throat, holding it tight.

Forest: Kids ever chase you, Les? With sticks and things?

Leslie: Let me go.

Forest: Some guy ever hold you down while another one burnt your face with a cigarette?

Leslie: This isn't funny.

Forest: Some stinking wino ever rape your ass in an alley?

Leslie: I can't breathe.

Forest: People ever call you names?

Leslie: Yes!

Forest: What names?

Leslie: Hairlip! Frog eyes! Scarface!

Forest: *Tightening rope around Leslie's throat.* Did it make you want to kill them?

Leslie: No.

Forest abruptly lets Leslie go, pushing him away.

Shaun Johnston as Forest, Jeff Hirschfield as Leslie.

Forest: You're a suck.

Leslie: Forest?

Forest: You have no pain. No anger.

Leslie: I do so.

Forest: You should think about the names they called you.

Leslie: Don't.

Forest: Think about the names, Suck!

Leslie: What's wrong?

Forest: Get out of my sight.

Pause. Leslie exits.

Forest: Veronica.

SCENE 41

Sabina's office. Morning. She is working. There is a knock at the door.

Sabina: Enter.

Lottie enters. She is in a very good mood.

Lottie: Mr. Forest to see you.

Sabina: Forest.

Lottie: Ma'am?

Sabina: Send him in.

Lottie exits. Forest enters.

Sabina: Yes?

Forest: I'm leaving.

Sabina: Why?

Forest: It's time.

Sabina: You're not running away from anything are you, Forest?

Forest: What would I be running from?

Sabina: Me. Veronica. Acker.

Forest: Acker's gone.

Sabina: Yes.

Forest: You don't need me anymore.

Sabina: When would you like to leave?

Forest: Tonight.

Sabina: I'll have your cheque ready this afternoon. Now, if you'll excuse me, I'm showing my new son-in-law his future domain this morning.

SCENE 42

Veronica's bedroom. Morning. Cole is nearly finished dressing. Veronica wakes.

Veronica: What do you think you're doing?

Cole: Meeting your mother. I'm late.

Veronica: But Cole, I want to...

Cole: *Cutting her off.* This is important.

There is a knock at the door.

Cole: Come in.

Lottie enters with a breakfast tray.

Lottie: Mr. Cole, you're not leaving before breakfast?

Cole: Afraid so. Lottie, what's that perfume you're wearing?

Lottie: Same stuff as always.

Cole: It's lovely.

Lottie: Goodbye, Mr. Cole.

Cole: Goodbye, Lottie.

Cole exits. Lottie takes the tray to Veronica.

Veronica: I don't want it!

Lottie: Yes'm.

Veronica: Did you cash that cheque I gave you?

Lottie: Yes.

Veronica: Good. I want you gone by the end of the week.

Lottie: What?

Veronica: Now go give Mother your notice.

Pause.

Lottie: No.

Veronica: What?

Lottie: If I go, Miss Veronica, you can be damn sure Mr. Cole and Miss Sabina will know what happened in this room last night.

Veronica: You wouldn't.

Lottie: And won't they want to know why. And won't I just tell them. You think I bought that cock-and-bull horseback story? You think I haven't seen you going out to the garage at night?

Veronica: I don't know what you're talking about.

Lottie: I know things, Miss Veronica. I know about the spook moving around this place. He's not strong enough for the others to see him yet, but I can. I know who he is.

Veronica: No one will believe you.

Lottie: I think certain people are getting suspicious already.

Veronica: You're horrible!

Pause.

Lottie: I like my job.

Veronica: Okay, okay.

Lottie: And something else.

Veronica: What?

Lottie: Mr. Cole liked that potion I made last night. I think he might want to try it again. Two or three times a week.

Veronica: You little slut!

Lottie smiles and exits. Veronica throws herself on the bed. Cole enters.

Cole: I got away.

Veronica: Fabulous.

Cole: Your mother seemed depressed.

Veronica: So what?

Cole: Forest told her he's leaving.

Veronica: He did what?!

Cole: Veronica, you don't even like him.

Veronica: I'm upset – for Momma.

Cole strokes her body.

Cole: Let's not worry about it.

Veronica: *Moving away from him.* Not now, Cole. I have too much to think about.

Cole: Like what?

Veronica: Like my life!

SCENE 43

The garage. Day. Forest is packing his bag. Leslie enters.

Leslie: Please don't leave. No one's ever made me feel the way you do.

Forest: Go away.

Leslie: Why?

Forest: Because I can't stand the sight of you.

Leslie: You said I was handsome.

Forest: I said whatever I had to to get you to bend over for me.

Leslie: I thought you liked me.

Forest suddenly reaches out and grabs Leslie's moustache, pulling it hard.

Forest: You're an ugly man, no matter how hard you try to hide it.

Leslie: That hurts.

Forest: You've got no guts, Suck!

Forest pushes Leslie away.

Leslie: Why are you so angry?

Forest: Get out.

Veronica enters. She is wearing a coloured dress.

Veronica: Leslie?

Leslie: What are you doing here?

Forest: Goodbye, Leslie.

Leslie exits quickly.

Veronica: What are you going to do about him?

Forest: Nice dress. White was definitely not your colour.

Forest does up his bag.

Veronica: Lottie knows everything.

Forest: So?

Veronica: She's a sort of witch. She was with Cole last night.

Forest: Great.

Veronica: She's blackmailing me so she can keep sleeping with my husband.

Forest: Good.

Veronica: You've got to kill her.

Forest: I'm leaving.

Veronica: Listen, you ugly bastard, she knows about Acker!

Forest: Then we're both in trouble.

Veronica: I never laid a hand on him.

Forest: It won't matter.

Veronica: Please.

Forest: Do it yourself. Get your handsome husband to help you.

Veronica: Don't be stupid.

Forest: I'll do it for a kiss.

Veronica: You know I can't do that.

Forest: You'll have to.

Veronica: Stop it.

Veronica slaps Forest hard across the face.

Forest: One kiss.

Veronica slaps Forest again.

Forest: And she's gone.

Veronica moves away from Forest.

Veronica: You put something in me. Some seed. Some disease.

Forest: I have nothing to do with what's inside of you.

Veronica: You'd kill her for a kiss.

Forest: Yes.

Veronica: Would you kill me for a kiss?

Forest: Yes.

Veronica: Why?

Pause.

Veronica: Why?

Forest: If I kill her, it means I'll have to stay.

Pause.

Veronica: *Quietly.* Yes.

Forest: I won't let you sleep with Cole.

Veronica: If that's what it takes.

Forest: Yes.

Veronica moves to Forest. She puts her arms around him and kisses him hard on the lips for a long moment. Forest puts his arms around her and holds her very tight. Veronica breaks away from him. Long pause. They do not look at one another.

Forest: Veronica.

Veronica: What?

Forest: I love you.

Long pause. They turn to one another. Forest begins to move to her. She motions for him to stop.

Veronica: Lottie first.

Forest: She's dead.

Veronica: And you're mine.

Forest: Forever.

Veronica: Yes.

Veronica exits.

Acker: *Off.* Revenge.

Forest: No, Acker. This time it's my turn.

There is a knock at the door. Forest opens it. Leslie enters.

Forest: What do you want?

Leslie: I love you.

Pause.

Leslie: I wanted you to know that. That's all. Do whatever you have to, but I want you to know I love you.

Leslie softly kisses Forest on the lips. Forest stares at Leslie as if in a trance.

Leslie: Forest?

Forest slowly begins to advance on Leslie, forcing him to back away.

Forest: You're not supposed to touch me like that.

Leslie: What?

Forest: No one's supposed to touch me like that.

Leslie: Forest?

Forest: You have no right to touch me like that.

Leslie: Don't.

Forest hits Leslie very hard in the face. Leslie falls to the floor.

Forest: You ugly freak!

Leslie: Forest. Please.

Forest violently spits into Leslie's face.

Forest: Ugly suck!

Forest exits.

Leslie: Please.

Acker's ghost appears at the edge of the light.

Acker: Revenge.

Leslie: What?

The skull rolls out of the darkness, stopping in front of Leslie.

Acker: Revenge.

Leslie: *Picking up skull.* Acker.

Acker: Revenge.

Leslie: Yes.

Leslie moves off into the shadows of the garage.

SCENE 44

The drawing-room. Night. Veronica, Cole, and Sabina are there. Lottie is serving coffee.

Sabina: Veronica?

Veronica: Yes, Momma?

Sabina: What were you doing out in the garage this afternoon?

Veronica: Have you been spying on me?

Sabina: I've been keeping my eyes open.

Veronica: Well, if you must know, I went out there to apologize to Forest. Because I wanted him to stay, Momma. I wanted him to stay for you. And he said he would. He's going to stay. For you.

Sabina: For me.

Lottie: More coffee, Miss Sabina?

Sabina: I might as well. Getting to sleep doesn't seem to be much of a problem lately.

Veronica: I'm so glad to hear that.

Sabina: Yes, I'm sure you are. Have you been dreaming about Acker too, Veronica?

Pause.

Sabina: Leslie thinks he's dead.

Veronica: Leslie's crazy.

Sabina: I don't think so.

Lottie: Coffee, Mr. Cole?

Cole: No thank you, Lottie.

Veronica: Momma, don't you think it's time Lottie turned in? She worked so hard at the wedding and everything.

Lottie: I don't mind, Miss Sabina.

Veronica: You look exhausted, poor thing.

Sabina: You may go, Lottie.

Lottie: Yes'm.

Veronica: Good night, Dear.

Short pause.

Lottie: Good night.

Lottie exits.

Cole: You look tired yourself, Miss Sabina.

Sabina: I am.

Veronica: Maybe it's time you thought about retiring.

Sabina: Maybe.

There is a muffled noise, off.

Cole: What was that?

Veronica: Oh – clumsy Lottie probably dropped something. I'll check on her.

Veronica exits.

Sabina: Did you ever hear the story about how my husband had an entire family burned while they slept because he thought they'd spoken to the cops about his drug smuggling?

Cole: I never heard that story.

Sabina: Of course no one could prove anything.

Cole: You okay?

Sabina: I've never been able to get it out of my mind. That woman and her children. Burning.

Cole: Pretty gross.

Sabina: Do all children pay for the crimes of their parents?

Cole: I don't know.

Sabina: Cole, when we're seeing Acker in our dreams, I don't think it's the trees he's pointing to. I think it's the forest.

Cole: You think Forest's got something to do with it?

Sabina: *Quietly.* I didn't think he was like other men.

Veronica has entered and heard the last of Sabina's speech. Sabina notices her.

Sabina: Why are you breathing so hard?

Veronica: The stairs.

Sabina: I see.

Veronica: Lottie's fine.

Sabina: I'm sure she is.

Cole: I think I'm ready for bed.

Veronica: Good night, Cole.

Cole: Do I get a kiss?

Veronica: Later. Good night.

Cole exits. Pause.

Veronica: Momma, have you got something on your mind?

Sabina: I have many things on my mind.

Pause.

Veronica: I'm tired too.

Sabina: Go to bed.

Veronica: Aren't you going to give me a kiss?

Pause.

Sabina: No.

Pause.

Veronica: I see. Good night, Mother.

Veronica exits.

SCENE 45

The garage. Night. Forest leads Lottie on. Her hands are bound with a long rope. Forest carries a letter Lottie has written.

Lottie: There, Mr. Forest. I wrote what you asked. Untie me now?

Forest: No.

Lottie: I'll go away. Just like I wrote. Promise.

Forest: No.

Lottie: I was – was just trying to teach Miss Veronica a lesson, that's all. I wouldn't've said anything. I swear.

Forest: No.

Lottie: This'll come back on you. Both of you!

There is a knock at the door. Forest gags Lottie and hobbles her ankles with the rope. Forest goes to the door.

Forest: Yes?

Veronica: Let me in.

Forest opens the door. Veronica enters carrying a small handgun.

Veronica: I brought a gun.

Forest: I don't need a gun.

Veronica: You never know.

Forest hands Veronica Lottie's note.

Veronica: "Dear Miss Sabina. Please forgive me for leaving you, but now that Miss Veronica's married my job is done. I want a life of my own. Thank you for everything. Lottie." Perfect.

Lottie struggles and tries to speak through the gag. Veronica produces a large amount of cash.

Veronica: The little fool hid the money I gave her in her room. I'll say she asked me for it so she could go away.

Forest: You don't miss a thing.

Lottie tries to plead again. Veronica slaps her.

Veronica: It's going to be hard training someone to replace her. Forest, Momma suspects.

Forest: What do you want to do?

Veronica: What do you think? Kill Lottie now. I want to watch.

Lottie struggles and protests.

Forest: In a hurry to get back to your pretty husband?

Veronica: Shut up and kill her.

Forest: Why don't you do it?

Veronica: Technically, I haven't killed anyone yet.

Forest: So commit.

Veronica: I'm lousy with a gun.

Forest produces a large utility knife and hands it to Veronica. She sets down the gun and takes the knife.

Forest: Do the jugular. You get a nice splash.

Veronica: I couldn't.

Forest: You could.

Veronica draws the blade across Lottie's throat. Lottie struggles and moans. There is a great spout of blood, covering Veronica's hands. Lottie shakes violently until she is dead. Veronica looks at her hands. She raises them to her nose and sniffs them. She tastes a bit of the blood.

Veronica: Salty.

Veronica grabs Forest and kisses him hard, driving her tongue into his mouth, smearing his face with blood. Acker appears at the edge of the light.

Acker: Revenge.

Veronica: Who's that?

Forest: Acker's ghost. He's harmless.

Veronica: How do we get rid of him?

Forest: I'll burn the skull. Then he can rest in peace.

Veronica: Good. We'll do it later. Let him watch if he wants.

Forest unties the rope from Lottie's wrists.

Forest: And now.

Veronica: The rope.

Forest: I tie you up...

Veronica: No.

Forest: What?

Veronica: Give me the rope.

Forest: What?

Veronica: Give it to me.

Forest gives Veronica the rope. She moves behind him and plays the rope around and across Forest's throat.

Veronica: I think it's my turn to tie you up.

Forest: Me?

Veronica: I do things to you. You like that idea?

Forest: Yes.

Veronica begins to tighten the rope around his neck. Forest gets on his knees. Veronica leads him about like a dog.

Veronica: Me too. You'll crawl on your knees. You'll grovel. You'll do whatever I tell you to. I'll treat you like the ugly, worthless pig you are.

Forest: Yes.

Veronica: You'll be my thing.

Forest: Yes.

Veronica: My slave.

Forest: We'll go away.

Veronica: *Letting go of the rope.* What?

Forest: To Europe. Africa. Russia.

Veronica: What are you talking about?

Forest: We'll be alone.

Veronica: And give up the ranch? The money?

Forest: We'll get by.

Veronica: I don't think so.

Forest: What?

Veronica: I'm staying right here. Where I belong.

Forest: I can't stay here. What if they come snooping around? People suspect.

Veronica: When that finally happens you are going to confess to everything. You did it all by yourself.

Forest: Veronica?...

Veronica: After all, it's what any man would do for the woman he loves.

Forest: You love me too!

Veronica: I never said that.

Forest: You didn't have to.

Veronica: Really Forest, how could someone like me ever love someone like you?

Forest: But the way you acted, the things you said...

Veronica: *Interrupting.* I said whatever I had to to get you to kill them for me.

Forest: Veronica, please don't.

Veronica: I'm surprised, Forest. I really didn't think you'd fall for it.

Forest: Please.

Veronica: But you really do love me, don't you?

Forest: Yes.

Veronica: You'll have to kill Momma too.

Forest: There's been too much killing already.

Veronica: Please, Forest – I was just starting to respect you.

Forest: You have to love me!

Veronica: Why?

Forest: Because – because you do! Because I need you! Because I want you to.

Veronica: I think you want a little too much, Forest.

Pause.

Veronica: And if and when you're caught you will admit to everything. Including Lottie.

Forest: Yes.

Veronica: Great. Now cheer up. It might be months before anyone catches on and there's a lot I want to do in the meantime. If it's any consolation I do enjoy the sex.

Pause.

Veronica: I'll be back later. Get Lottie out of here before she starts to smell.

Forest: Please don't leave me.

Veronica: What? I can hardly hear you.

Forest: Please don't leave me, Veronica.

Veronica: But Forest, I have to.

Forest: Don't leave me alone.

Veronica: Beg.

Forest: Please.

Veronica: Beg.

Forest: Don't leave me! I love you!

Veronica laughs.

Veronica: Oh yes, you definitely wanted too much this time. Don't worry. I'll be back later. I'll put the gun...

Veronica stops abruptly as she realizes the gun is gone.

Veronica: Where's the gun?

Leslie enters from the shadows, carrying the gun. He has shaved his moustache.

Leslie: I've got it.

Forest: Leslie.

Leslie: You killed him. Both of you.

Veronica: Leslie, it was lies. All lies! He made me say those things.

Leslie: Shut up! *To Forest.* You used me.

Forest: Yes.

Leslie: I was too ugly.

Forest: No Les, you weren't ugly enough.

Leslie: You wanted her all along!

Forest: Yes.

Leslie: You love *her*!!

Forest: She's like me.

Veronica: He's lying!

Leslie: Murderers.

Veronica: You didn't exactly rush out here to save Lottie.

Leslie: I didn't kill her. I didn't kill Acker.

Acker appears at the edge of the light.

Veronica: Nothing will ever bring him back, Leslie.

Acker: Revenge.

Veronica: All you can do is burn the skull and release him.

Acker: Revenge.

Forest: She's lying, Les. He won't rest until we've both paid for our crimes.

Veronica: Shut up!

Acker: Revenge.

Forest: You have to do it, Les.

Veronica: Don't listen to him.

Forest: You have to do us both.

Veronica: Don't!

Forest: Kill us!

Veronica: Leslie.

Forest: We killed your brother.

Veronica: He did it all!

Leslie aims the gun at Veronica.

Leslie: You don't fool me, Veronica.

Veronica: You wouldn't dare shoot me.

Leslie: Wouldn't I?

Leslie cocks the gun.

Forest: No!

Forest rushes at Leslie. Leslie turns and shoots Forest in the knee. Forest screams and falls.

Leslie: She used you!

Veronica: Leslie, listen, there's a – a lot of money involved here. Money we could share. Money –

Leslie: Shut up!

Forest: Don't hurt her.

Veronica: Please!

Leslie: You bitch!

Veronica: Please, Leslie. Please don't kill me. I'll do anything.

Leslie: I'm going to kill you both, Veronica.

Forest rises and hobbles toward Leslie.

Forest: Yes. We both deserve it.

Leslie: You're right.

Forest: Kill us.

Leslie shoots Forest in the other knee. Forest screams and falls to the ground clutching his leg.

Leslie: I am an ugly man.

Veronica: What are you doing?

Leslie: A very ugly man.

Forest: Kill us!

Veronica: No!

Sabina and Cole burst in.

Sabina: Veronica!

Cole: Jesus!

Veronica runs to Sabina and Cole.

Veronica: Oh Momma! Momma! Stop him. He's going to hurt me. I didn't do anything. I swear I didn't. Forest made me! He did horrible things to me. He –

Veronica trails off as she realizes that Cole and Sabina are looking from Lottie's body to the blood on her hands. Veronica puts her bloodied hands behind her back.

Sabina: *To Forest.* What did you do to us?

Leslie: Nothing we didn't deserve.

Sabina: I trusted you.

Forest: I did what I was taught, Sabina.

Cole: You were sleeping with him?

Veronica: He made me.

Leslie: Stand away from them, Veronica.

Veronica: Momma, please –

Leslie: Stand away.

Veronica moves away from Sabina and Cole.

Veronica: Leslie, this won't change anything.

Leslie: *To Forest. Ignoring her.* I thought you didn't love me because you didn't need love. I thought you were strong.

Veronica: He's as weak as the rest of you.

Leslie: Careful, Veronica.

Sabina: Leslie, I sent Sam for the sherriff when I heard the first shot –

Leslie: Good.

Veronica: Go ahead and kill me! I don't think you've got the guts. I think you're as weak and stupid as everyone else here. I think you're worse because you're so ugly. You're all ugly. You're all ugly –

Leslie shoots Veronica in the head. She falls.

Forest: No!

Sabina: Veronica!

Cole: Jesus.

Forest: Please kill me.

Sabina goes to Veronica. She kneels and looks at the body, but doesn't touch it. Leslie aims the gun at Forest's head.

Forest: Do it.

Acker's ghost reappears at the edge of the light.

Acker: Revenge.

Cole: Jesus.

Short pause, then Leslie lowers the gun.

Leslie: I don't think so.

Forest: What?

Leslie: Miss Sabina, Forest's decided to stay. He's going to stay for a long, long time.

Sabina: What?

Forest: No. I won't.

Leslie: Trust me. You will.

Cole: Leslie – ?

Leslie: I'm fine Cole, thanks.

Sabina: You're not going to get away with this.

Leslie: Sure I will. I killed your daughter for killing my brother and your maid. I'll go to trial, but no one in the county will blame me for what I did. Veronica killed them both.

Sabina: That's not true.

Leslie: It is now. Isn't it, Cole?

Pause.

Cole: Sure.

Sabina: They'll never believe you.

Leslie: They will if everyone backs me up. And if everyone doesn't I think it makes them, at least, an accessory to murder. Unless, of course, you honestly didn't suspect anything, Miss Sabina.

Pause.

Leslie: You're an intelligent woman.

Sabina: *To Forest.* I thought you were different.

Forest: I'll tell the cops the truth. I will...

Leslie: No, Forest. You're going to spend some time somewhere where no one can see or hear you. There must be a place like that on this ranch. Does anything occur to you, Miss Sabina? Somewhere where Forest can suffer by himself.

Sabina rises from Veronica's body. She stares at it as she thinks, then looks at Forest with great hatred.

Sabina: The root cellar.

Leslie: Perfect.

Forest: Sabina, you can't let him do this.

Sabina: Yes I can.

Forest: You're talking about your own daughter.

Sabina: You ruined her.

Forest: Veronica was ruined when I got here.

Sabina: I just wanted to protect her.

Leslie: You know Cole, I think we're going to like it here.

Cole: We are?

Leslie: The way I see it, you're Miss Sabina's only surviving heir. And she's very tired. She's lost her only daughter. She has very little to live for. You'd inherit everything.

Cole: That's right.

Leslie: Wouldn't you agree, Miss Sabina?

Short pause.

Sabina: Yes.

Leslie: Why don't you lie down until the sheriff gets here. You look awfully tired and he's going to have a lot of questions.

Sabina: Yes.

Leslie: It's going to be hard – answering all those questions.

Leslie hands Sabina the gun.

Leslie: Why don't you take this. In case you have trouble sleeping.

After a moment Sabina takes the gun.

Sabina: Yes.

Forest: Sabina.

Sabina looks at Forest for a moment.

Sabina: I'm so tired.

Sabina exits.

Acker: Revenge.

Cole: *Referring to Acker.* How long is he staying?

Leslie: Until Forest's dead.

Cole: Hey Les, I didn't mean what I said before. If you want we could...

Leslie: *Cutting him off.* I do. Later. Go to the house.

Cole: Whatever you say.

Cole begins to move from the garage. A loud shot is heard off. Cole stops and looks at Leslie. Leslie gives Cole a reassuring smile. Cole exits to the house.

Acker: Revenge.

Forest: Listen to him.

Acker: Revenge.

Leslie: Don't worry. He'll get his revenge.

Forest: Kill me.

Leslie: Eventually.

Forest: My legs....

Leslie: Yes. We've got to do something about that.

Forest: Hurts.

Leslie: Well, the kneecaps are shattered.

Forest: Please.

Leslie: A doctor might be able to do something about them but that's not a possibility right now. We don't want you running away.

Forest: Kill me.

Leslie exits into the darkness.

Acker: Revenge.

Forest: Veronica.

Forest drags himself to Veronica and cradles her body.

Acker: Revenge.

Forest: Veronica!

Leslie enters carrying the axe and an acetylene torch.

Leslie: Let her go.

Forest puts Veronica down and moves slightly away from the body.

Forest: Jesus, Leslie – no.

Leslie moves toward Forest. He lights the torch and sterilizes the axe.

Forest: Don't. Please.

Forest: Please!

Leslie kicks Forest's legs apart, wide. Forest screams in pain.

Leslie: This is going to hurt a lot. But I want you to be very very quiet.

Forest: No.

Leslie hefts the axe in his hand.

Leslie: Be very very quiet.

Acker: Revenge!

Leslie suddenly brings the axe over his head, aiming it directly at Forest's leg. The lights snap to black.

Afterword

by Gerry Potter[*]

As Paula Simons has pointed out so compellingly in the Foreword, much of the humour in *The Ugly Man*, and a large part of the play's accessibility, derives from the pop culture worlds of film and television. But pop cult alone does not explain the power of the piece to keep audiences riveted to their seats and gasping for breath. Nor does it account for the play's extraordinary resonance of the playwright's ideas and passions. To understand the source of these strengths, we must look to Brad Fraser's longtime immersion in the world of theatre.

While most of that immersion has been with new play companies, particularly in western Canada, the original inspirations for *The Ugly Man* were, oddly enough, classical. Fraser first embarked on the creation of his play during a summer at Stratford, Ontario, while his partner of the time was acting in the Festival Theatre's Young Company, working on Middleton and Rowley's *The Changeling*. The main plot of this Jacobean tragicomedy, in which a young noblewoman, at first repulsed by the ugly servant DeFlores, later gets his help in murdering the fiancé her father has chosen for her, gave Fraser his main storyline, including the two plotters' spiralling descent into the maelstrom of adultery, blackmail, and murder. The Jacobean plot also gave Fraser three of his funnier episodes: the virginity potion test, the bed trick, in

---

[*] Gerry Potter is Artistic Director of Workshop West Theatre, Edmonton.

which a lusty serving woman switches places with her mistress in the bridal bed, and the appearance of a vengeful ghost.

Of course, Fraser has also radically transformed the original classic. He has deleted characters, added and altered others, dropped the entire subplot and suggested new and telling motivations for the evil done by the two central characters. In suggesting that Veronica's and Forest's perverse horrors may be a response to repression or abuse inflicted upon them by others, Fraser identifies some of the specific evils with which he is concerned: our current society's materialism, sexual repression, intolerance, and obsession with a particular idea of beauty. Beyond this suggestion of societal responsibility, Fraser goes much further than Middleton and Rowley in exploring the twisted relationship between the two central characters; he also creates an abusive relationship between Forest and Leslie. In both relationships the tables are eventually turned, with Forest the abuser becoming Forest the abused. Here lies Fraser's central theme, and the one closest to his own heart: the accelerating cycles by which abuse is passed from one relationship, or from one generation, to the next.

If Fraser borrows from a classic drama for his story, he also displays another tenet of the dramatic tradition in *The Ugly Man*: the primacy of dramatic action. Fraser has learned, more likely from theatre audiences than from Aristotle's *Poetics*, the skills of a master storyteller, who knows how to drive a story by its characters' obsessions and passions. In this play he employs nearly all the storyteller's techniques: suspense, humour, irony, surprise, magic, horror, and, of course, sex and stylized violence. There are no long monologues or speeches, no debates; characters don't talk about the issues, they simply act. *The Ugly Man*'s themes are embedded in and demonstrated by the action. This is classic playwriting. The irony is that this dynamism also explains some of the play's appeal to a youthful audience brought up on *Star Trek* reruns, *Friday the 13th* and Madonna videos.

Brad Fraser should know the medium of theatre well. He has been working in live theatre since his days in Performing Arts at Edmonton's Victoria Comp High, when, as the high school winner in the provincial playwriting contest, he rubbed shoulders with members of the Banff Centre Playwrights' Colony. During that period he also worked with the community theatre, Walterdale, whose board he scandalized twice, first by doing a scene from *Zastrozzi* in the nude, later by directing his own play about angry teens, *Mutants*, in 1981. In the early 1980s he spent several years in Toronto, mostly working with Paul Thompson at Theatre Passe Muraille, before returning west and teaming up with Workshop West Theatre and later, Alberta Theatre Projects.

His recent plays have been extensively workshopped and revised. *Unidentified Human Remains and the True Nature of Love*, for example, began at Workshop West in 1985 as a series of actor improvisations on the subject of friendship, meant to provide a springboard for Fraser's writing. By the time it was workshopped nearly two years later at the conclusion of a residency at Workshop West, only faint traces of the original improvisations remained. Then Fraser and the play went through two more years of residency and workshops at ATP, prior to its première there.

The Ugly Man also had a series of workshops at Workshop West, and later, the Banff Centre, prior to its production at ATP and the subsequent production under Fraser's direction at Workshop West. In this signature production, the author/director revelled in the play's heightened theatricality, using visual selectivity and exaggeration, a highly charged soundscape including horrific live effects, and a frantic pace with many overlapping scenes.

The heightening became virtually surreal at times. For example, Veronica's wedding dress accessory, created by designer David Skelton, was a barbed wire cage around her neck and mouth; and blood spewed from an onstage fountain when Lottie's throat is slashed. Skelton's other costume designs were almost as bizarre: variations on corsets and heavy Kabuki-look make-up that underlined the repressiveness, obsession with control, and superficiality of the play's world. Lighting choices were extreme, with the first Forest-Veronica sex scene lit only by lightning flashes. Overall, the production basked in the sheer physicality of the theatre. In the tongue-in-cheek summary of reviewer Colin MacLean (after a long list of the play's comic and lurid physical delights): "in short, everything you could want from an evening of theatre."

Brad Fraser is, without doubt, a phenomenally gifted and skilled playwright, with a ready command of pop cult imagery. He also has a reputation as the bad boy of Canadian theatre, challenging the theatre establishment's political correctness, complacency, and failure to connect with young audiences. Nevertheless he is very much a man of the theatre, a product, not only of his difficult family life and his generation, but of years of experience with the medium. Moreover, he would not have developed as a playwright without the skill and support provided by the new play theatres with which he has worked. More specifically, he is one among an extraordinary group of Edmonton playwrights, including Frank Moher, Stewart Lemoine, Raymond Storey, Conni Massing, and Janet Hinton, who have learned the ropes at companies like Theatre Network, Workshop West, and the Edmonton Fringe, and who are making their mark on Canadian theatre.

It would be irresponsible not to point out the additional irony that, just at the time these playwrights are approaching their full power as mature artists, and some, like Brad Fraser, are garnering international attention, the theatres in which they trained are threatened as never before. Economic recession, competition from commercial megamusicals, threats of censorship, and severe government funding cuts are pushing these companies to the brink of collapse. And we move ever closer to the ugly world of *The Ugly Man*.

Edmonton
April, 1993

Biography

Playwright Brad Fraser, born in Edmonton in 1959, began winning Alberta Culture Playwriting competitions when he was a 17 year old student in theatre arts at Victoria Composite High School. For two summers he attended the Banff Centre Playwrights' Colony, headed by Sharon Pollock. He wrote and directed his first staged play, *Mutants*, solicited for the 1980-81 season by Walterdale Theatre Associates, Edmonton's community theatre, where he was also an actor, set designer, and stage manager. The following season, 25th Street Theatre, Saskatoon premièred *Wolfboy*, with further productions at Theatre Network, Edmonton; Touchstone Theatre, Vancouver; and Theatre Passe Muraille, Toronto. Two other works were performed at Passe Muraille: *Rude Noises (for a Blank Generation)*, a collective creation with Paul Thompson in 1982, and *Young Art* in 1986. Fraser subsequently wrote *Chainsaw Love* (1985) and *The Return of the Bride* (1988) for the Edmonton Fringe Festival.

In 1986, Fraser became resident playwright at Edmonton's Workshop West Theatre. Here began *Unidentified Human Remains and the True Nature of Love*, premièred in Calgary at Alberta Theatre Projects' playRites 1989. With this play Fraser achieved national and international recognition with productions in Toronto, Edmonton, Montreal, Chicago, New York, Milan, Edinburgh, London, and Tokyo. The movie version, adapted by the playwright and directed by Denys Arcand, was released in 1993. For three seasons Fraser wrote and/or directed plays for the Edmonton Teen Festival at the Citadel Theatre: Jeffrey Hirschfield's *Blood Brothers* (1989); a revised *Young Art* (1990); and *Prom Night of the Living Dead*, with music by Darrin Hagen (1991). Release of a film version of *Prom Night* is pending. *The Ugly Man* was premièred at playRites 1992 with subsequent productions in Montreal and Edmonton. The French version, (*L'homme laid*), directed by Derek Goldby at Théâtre de Quat'Sous, was published in spring 1993. The French translation of *Human Remains (Des restres humains non-identifiés et la véritable nature de l'amour)* is scheduled for publication in fall 1993.

Fraser's most recent work includes a musical version of the Craig Russell movie, *Outrageous*, in collaboration with Darrin Hagen and Andy Northrup, and a play, *Poor Superman*, to be produced in Cincinnati in winter 1994.